MISERY IN MINISTRY

KECIA C. TAYLOR

CONTENTS

Foreword	ix
Demons of the Past	1
The Naked Conference	5
Locked Up Love	15
Get Through the Night	19
Abandonment	47
Daddy Issues	53
Sanity over Accolades	69
Broken Promises	79
Favor	91
Demons Resurfaced	105
Therapy: A New Beginning	117
Final Thoughts	123

Misery in Ministry
Copyright © 2020 by Kecia C. Taylor

Published by: Diamond Publishing, LLC
Email: info@diamondpublishingllc.com

All rights reserved. This book or any portion thereof
may not be reproduced or used in any manner whatsoever without the express written permission of the publisher except for the use of brief quotations in a book review.

Book Creation & Design:
DHBonner Virtual Solutions
www.dhbonner.net

ISBN 978-0-578-72073-9

Printed in the United States of America

First Printing, 2020

DEDICATED TO...

My husband:
Milton C. Taylor

My mother:
Edith E. Dixon

My grandmother:
Bessie M. Jiles

My siblings:
Jonathan, John, Veronica, Patrick, and Taiheisha

My forever sister friends:
Paris and Greta

My sister from another Mama:
Claudette

My sons:
Jonathan, Malachi, and Ezra

*"I'm too real to be fake,
and too flawed to be phony."*

-Kecia C. Taylor

FOREWORD

The first time I sat at the feet of Kecia, she was Evangelist Kecia Sims, a guest teacher at my church who talked about the different elements of prayer. I was fascinated with Kecia because she was beautiful, a passionate speaker, carried a great presence when she entered the room, and was transparent about herself. She talked about her experience coming to our church that day, remembering many years prior that she left that general neighborhood to escape from a violent marriage, and she was amazed that she returned to the same neighborhood teaching about prayer. Who does that? Who talks about real issues like that and carries a title in a church? After that encounter, I became a great admirer of Kecia and wanted to connect with her in some way, somehow.

Years later, I followed her on Myspace (and yes, I am dating myself) and found myself sitting at her feet again, visiting her church as she was now Pastor Kecia. The awe of this woman never stopped amazing me as she can preach souls out of hell and have all of heaven shouting at the powerful messages that she consistently gives.

Over time, Kecia became my spiritual mentor and teacher as she stretched me and challenged me to walk in the gifts that God has placed in me as a minister. She welcomed my profession as a licensed marriage and family therapist/psychotherapist, and also promoted my private practice, Heaven Sent Consultation, and encouraged mental health issues to be a welcomed topic in her sermons and bible studies. Kecia always talked about how the churches need to stop being so "churchy" and address real issues plaguing the people in the church.

Being on Pastor Kecia's ministerial team, I have seen her minister to, pray for, and speak over countless people while dealing with her own personal crisis and challenges. As her minister, I felt it was not my place to speak to her about her challenges because Kecia was the shepherd entrusted with a flock God gave her; plus, she had her family, close friends, and spiritual coverings. But one afternoon following a church service, all that changed. Pastor Kecia called me to her office and sat me down and told me many of the things she was battling with. As I listened to her, I didn't see Kecia, the Pastor. I didn't see Kecia, the powerhouse preacher, nor Kecia, the spiritual mentor to many. I saw Kecia, the woman.

As she removed her robe as pastor and preacher, I put on my psychotherapist hat and friend and saw a woman who ministered to so many broken people that she, herself, was broken. I saw a woman who encouraged transparency in the pulpit cut her heart open in order for me to see the pain she was dealing with. And I remember telling her, "you have taken care of so many people, it's now time to take care of you." She then told me she was seeing a therapist, and my response? "Good for you! It is definitely good for church folks to know they can have Jesus and a therapist too."

I am so proud of the journey I took with Kecia sitting at her feet, learning about ministry, transparency, and when to let go and let God take care of you. She has helped so many people deal with their issues while dealing with her personal trauma, and I wonder how many more will she help while she is standing in the light of God's healing.

The saying goes, "misery loves company." Still, I hope this book will begin a journey for a company of pastors, preachers, and ministers to begin the journey of their own healing and being transparent about their own struggles and challenges so that those they minister to can be liberated to address their own pain. It is reported that one in four people in the world will be affected by a mental or neurological disorder at some point in their lives.

So, I hope this book will teach church folks that mental health can happen to anyone regardless of title, ethnicity, race, marital status, financial status, neighborhood, and faith. And it can happen to pastors, too. Mental health is not taboo. Healing

FOREWORD

starts when you can take that brave step and acknowledge that there is a problem.

Carmel T Ross Owolabi, LMFT
www.heavensentconsult.com

DEMONS OF THE PAST

I was standing at the stove cooking dinner when I heard a familiar voice coming from my husband's phone. He had been scrolling through videos on Facebook or YouTube like he normally does. But this voice caught my attention. He had clicked on a sermon I preached several years ago. With my back still to him as if I were eavesdropping, I listened to my deep, powerful preacher voice.

Through the phone I began to exclaim, "You weren't there with me in the midnight hour." "You weren't there when I felt alone." "And you weren't there when I took the sleeping pills and drank alcohol and got on the highway and drove my car across town." "You weren't there!" With each declaration of the anguish about people not being there when I was suffering, my voice became louder and stronger.

That sermon was many years ago. However, at that

moment, it hit me, and I said out loud, "I've had issues for a long time." I was embarrassed. I was ashamed. At that moment, in the privacy of my home — with my husband there — I stood with my head down, pretending to stir the pot, and I was ashamed. There are at least two sermons of me preaching that you can find where I wanted to make a plan to commit suicide.

I should have sought help so much sooner than I did. All the signs were there. I had been haunted by this spirit for years and just didn't take it seriously. The truth of the matter is, I didn't know what was happening to me. Later in life, I found out that family members suffered from nervous breakdowns and other mental health issues. These were issues that had an impact on their lives, but it didn't necessarily stop them from living productive lives. If these things were discussed more openly, perhaps I wouldn't have suffered the way I did. I was left thinking my issues with contemplating suicide were because I wasn't living Godly enough and that if I just made up my mind to completely walk with God, I wouldn't have these feelings.

Growing up in church, I never heard about therapy or mental health issues. If you had a problem in your life, you were supposed to take it to Jesus. Taking it to Jesus meant going to church and praying. At least that was the only answer I was given in my younger years. I didn't know how to "take it to Jesus." Was I supposed to hand Him my problem like I would hand someone a piece of paper? I just didn't know what it meant, and the preaching and teaching of that day was less about ministering to the person and more about telling you what you could and couldn't do to be saved and go to heaven. The only way I knew how to deal with problems was to go to church and cry out, shout, and dance. The euphoric high you get when leaving a good church service would mask the pain for a day or two, but the internal bruises and the root of the issues weren't addressed. When problems aren't addressed, they tend to come back harder and stronger.

Allow me to take you on a journey that almost cost my life. A journey full of twists, turns, love, compassion, bad decisions, and mistakes that changed my life forever.

THE NAKED CONFERENCE

THE DREAM: As I entered the dark room, the red and blue strobe lights were reflecting from wall to wall. I wasn't familiar with the song or music, but the young people who were performing were extremely animated. In fact, I really couldn't even hear the music, but there was definitely music playing. There was a certain rhythm and vibe in the room. I just couldn't hear the sound.

There was a stage where young people were performing. The seating was off as well. There were tables and chairs. There were also sofas against the walls with little round tables in front of them. As I was walked in to find a seat, men were carrying in more tables and chairs to add to the confusion of the atmosphere. The event had already started, but the room wasn't fully set up. There were quite a few people in the room, and they were engaged in the performance. Still looking for a seat in the dark, the only comfort I had was my one-hundred-and-fifty-pound Italian Mastiff, Ezra, who was walking by my side.

Ezra is very protective, so much so that he doesn't like anyone to get too close to each other, making sure that no one is hurting anyone else. He is especially protective of his Mommy. He's a big boy, weighing in at close to 150 pounds, although he was only fourteen months (at the time of this dream). His beautiful formentino coat accents his bright hazel eyes, and his facial characteristics are strong and intense; he looks quite serious and sometimes intimidating. Ezra can be the sweetest puppy but turns into a savage protector when he feels his family is threatened. There is no way I would have taken him in a public place so chaotic, dark, and full of people he didn't know, but there he was, in my dream, right by my side.

We find an empty corner spot. Victoria, my twenty-year-old niece, happened to be there, so I took a seat next to her, and Ezra lies next to me. I'm comforted, but I'm confused. I know churches cater to millennials these days, but the atmosphere just didn't seem right, even for the new-age type of worship services. I may be pushing fifty, but I am by no means an old fogy. I understand meeting the young people where they are and providing a worship experience that they can relate to. But the environment felt more like a lounge than a church service, worship experience, or God encounter. Whatever they are calling it these days, this wasn't it.

As I try to engage in the "praise dancers" from the lounge-like leather sofa, I noticed that someone was hovering over my shoulder. This was strange because the couch was against the wall. I turned around, and to my disgust, a young chubby boy was sitting on the back of the sofa completely naked! "What the hell are you doing?" I snapped at him. Yes, we were in the "church," "worship experience," "God encounter" place, but he was naked, and his little fat junk was at eye level. In my disgust, I stood up and said, "Binkie, watch Ezra," and I walked out (Binkie is what we call my niece). I wasn't concerned about her safety because Ezra is just as protective of her as he is of me. She also knows how to handle him, so I knew they would be safe with each other. As I walked away, Ezra didn't budge. He just laid there, continuing to look at the performers.

Leaving the dark room, my eyes had to adjust when I walked into the corridor. At that point, I realized I was at a church conference. I'm sure I've attended hundreds in my lifetime, so the scenery was very familiar. It was a typical hotel corridor. The carpet was a lattice print in dark burgundy with gold accents. The feel of the plush carpet under my feet gave me confidence as I briskly walked away from the little chubby boy. Having attended so many church conferences while wearing heels, you get used to the different feel of walking on slippery lobby floors or concrete auditorium floors as opposed to walking on the plush carpet. You can walk a little more relaxed and upright on the carpet.

The walls were bright with big chandeliers glistening off the huge mirrors hanging on the walls. The carpet was the basic brown with gold emblems and designs as accents. As I walked down the hallway, I realized there was another "service" going on. I assumed it was the adult service. That was something common in my youth when I attended church conferences. The young people would have a room, and the adults would have a separate room adjacent to that room with a thick partition to separate the services. My assumption was spot on. This was the room for the adults. I started seeing adults gathering and walking into the room. They were congregating in the hall, greeting each other, laughing, and talking. The smiles on their faces indicated they were quite comfortable with each other and were excited to be in attendance. I, on the other hand, was very out of place and found myself in utter disgust and confusion again. "Why is everybody naked?" In my head, I'm saying the most sarcastic and colorful words, but I keep my mouth shut and just kept walking through the crowd. I was fully clothed, I might add!

After seeing grown men and women very naked and unashamed, I honestly don't know why I didn't go back and get my dog and leave. Maybe I didn't want to fight the little chubby kid. Oddly, his nakedness was the only one that offended me. Maybe it was because he had invaded my personal space. Maybe it was the invasion of my space, his nakedness, and the fact that he was sitting on the back of the couch. That was insulting to me as a mother. That boy acted like he had no home training! And I have a low tolerance for kids who display bad manners.

As I continued to journey down the hallway, I saw the

bishops! The grand bishops in their fine liturgical bishopric garb. White robes that flowed to the floor, black and red sashes laying neatly around their necks. It was impressive. This was the only sight of this conference that was reassuring. I had left the kids club lounge service, walked past the adult pre-porn gathering, so the sight of the bishops was refreshing. It was as if the grandparents were there and they were going to set all the children in order! What a relief! I noticed as I walked closer to them, the hallway was no longer carpeted. My steps became more cautious and careful. I didn't want to disturb them because they looked so serious, and a sense of reverence overcame me. Out of respect, I walked slowly, quietly, and cautiously because I didn't want to slip and fall in the presence of the bishops.

They were laughing as they lined up for their entrance into their grand ballroom. They were to my left. I could only see about ten of them, but it was apparent there were many more that hadn't walked out of their gathering place. There was one bishop who stood directly in front of me. He was standing by some glass doors that served as an entrance or exit to that part of the hotel. At the time, I only saw male bishops. However, a female bishop appeared at the door. The door was locked, and she was trying to open it. She was trying to get the bishop's attention. I didn't speak, but I was looking at him as if to say *dude, open the door!* I guess that's where I lost respect, even if it was only a thought. He wouldn't open the door. She knocked and called his name. He still didn't open it and then proceeded to reprimand her for being late and telling her how she doesn't respect protocol, and she should have been there on time.

I stood there stunned. Shocked. Irritated. Pissed off. Of all the madness that's going on at this conference, I couldn't believe his main concern was tardiness and protocol to the point he wouldn't let her in. How could he treat a fellow minister, bishop, and servant of the cloth in this manner? She was reprimanded like a child. He didn't bother to ask why she was late. He just chastised her. I guess I had enough of the foolishness. Where's Ezra? I just want my dog, and I'm out! This is where my dream ended.

This was an actual dream I had in January 2019. Over the course of three or four weeks, I had repeated dreams about church conferences. In the dreams, I am an adult, but the feeling was very nostalgic. Perhaps I was dreaming of how church used to be for me. Perhaps my subconscious has been longing for the experience of true fellowship and love. Perhaps in the depths of my soul, I've been yearning for the times when I would see people I loved from all over the country, and they were happy to see me. Perhaps I'm hungry for the days of church conferences before I ever experienced the other side of ministry. I guess that's why they call it a dream. In my subconscious, I fantasized about a time when I was happy about church gatherings and ministry.

The Dream Interpretation: When I told my husband about my dream, his response was, "You know you just described the condition of the church?" I felt that was the case, and he was the confirmation I needed. The dream was so vivid, but shockingly it wasn't disturbing. I guess because I've already accepted what I've been witnessing in the church environment over the past decade. I want to stress that I feel there are issues in the church "environment" and not God's church. I still believe God's word is true. I still believe His church is perfect. However, I do believe that many of the church environments created by flawed humans are far from perfect, and that is what this dream represented.

The three phases of my dream speak to the division in the church. We see churches catering to the youth while ignoring the wisdom of the elders. I'm not referring to the preachers or ministers, but I mean the elders who have more life experience who can share and impart wisdom based on their failures and successes in life. The elders and their needs are often pushed to the background (except when their money is needed). Young people are used, promoted, and pushed to the forefront in ministry because they can gather more young people and tend to be more influential, especially if they can market their church as cool and not boring.

The nakedness of the adult service represents the sexual perversion that has infiltrated the churches. It's common for preachers to sleep with parishioners whether they are married or not. It's becoming more common to hear of the rape of men, women, and boys and girls by leaders in the church. Molestation of young children by pastors and bishops are flooding the headlines more and more. Sex in the actual sanctuary has also been known to happen.

The pompous actions of the bishops represented the "good ole boys" club that still exists in the church. Although women preachers and bishops have finally been acknowledged, they are not fully accepted. A lot of women are used as that "token" minority, so an organization can say, "See, we have one in our group." Overall, many church organizations are still very sexist and misogynistic.

People who choose to attend church, do so for fellowship, guidance, and a place to worship with like-minded people. The expectation when going to church is to be uplifted, encouraged, and to leave with a word from God to help live a better life. Many times, we hear, "Don't leave the way you came." But if the environment isn't a place of refuge or healing, oftentimes, people leave the same way they came or feeling worse. We should never leave a church service feeling worse than we did when we came. In this day, people are hurting and dealing with serious issues.

In 2020, we are dealing with a pandemic, social distancing, historic unemployment rates, police brutality, and blatant racism. The face of ministry has drastically changed. Due to the pandemic, churches have been closed, and pastors have had to adjust how they minister and serve their congregants. Many have recently realized they are no longer the "shot caller," but now they have to serve the people. The catchphrases and fancy suits with the assistance of a skilled musician to set the tone for the service are no longer valid. Pastors have to actually minister to people to help them survive this crazy time we live in.

While the pandemic has devastated our world, it is a blessing in disguise. It's caused families to spend more time together, marriages to reassess their priorities, and ministries to give concrete lessons from the Bible. A "name it and claim it" sermon won't work today. Prophesying a house or a car won't work during this pandemic. A family dealing with their loved one being killed by the police needs something more solid than telling them to give a one hundred dollar offering for a miracle. People are hurting and on the brink of losing their minds. They are turning to God and His chosen leaders for answers and guidance. What are we going to say to them? What are we going to tell them? What about those who were already dealing with demons from the past and then lost their job during the pandemic?

All of the traveling to revivals, conferences, and conventions has ceased. We're in a season where pastors have to pay attention to the congregants. They expect the tithes and offerings to continue to come in. Some even asked for people to tithe on the stimulus money that the government issued. Pastors still want their income. Well, if they still want you to fund the church and ministry, then make them earn it! Put a demand on the ministry. The days of being underserved in ministry are over. Don't go another day underserved in a ministry or fellowship. If you are supporting a pastor, bishop, church, ministry, or fellowship with your time, talents, and treasure (money), then you should be able to benefit as well. If the ministry doesn't know how to help you, don't feel bad about going to a different one. If you had an issue in your physical heart, would you continue to go to a doctor who didn't know how to help you? Or would you go to another doctor with experience and skill who could treat your ailment? You could have joined a church with a pre-existing condition. We all have baggage and issues. But if you aren't getting the help you need to heal in those areas, don't feel guilty about finding another place of worship.

I know about serving while hurting and not getting the help I needed. I progressed and moved up the ranks in ministry, but I did it with unresolved issues. It's easy to be more concerned with pursuing your purpose while denying your pain. People see the glamour of your progress, and they cheer you on. However, it's the gruesome details of your pain that is hidden that haunts you. If left unattended, you can function on a high level and be a blessing to thousands of people while you silently suffer in misery.

LOCKED UP LOVE

FOR A FEW MONTHS, I HOSTED A RADIO SHOW CALLED *Out of Bounds with Kecia*. It was an Internet radio show with a few hundred listeners where I talked about relationships. It was fun for the few months I hosted the show. The producer wanted it to be sports-themed, where we called fouls on relationship "plays." He also set the show up to where I was called a relationship strategist. I was never comfortable with that term. I never felt like I was qualified to walk in that "calling." I know in this day everybody wants to be a "life coach" just because of their personal experiences or trials of life. But unless you have gone to school for it or earned a certification, I think it's pretty bogus to deem yourself a life coach.

Well, I'm certainly no life coach. And truth be told, I could probably benefit from having one. I'm not writing this time in my life to proclaim a victory. It also isn't an acceptance of defeat. The purpose of including this experience is two-fold. One is to bring clarity to one of the hardest times of my life, specifically shedding light on the events of December 21, 2013. And the second reason is to save my own life. I guess there is a third reason as well. This is my admission of a mistake that I made. If anything, once you read this book, learn from my mistakes, and DON'T do what I did. It wasn't necessary for loved ones, friends, or enemies to say, "I told you so." I can look back and clearly see the reasons why I shouldn't be in this situation, but here I am in it. Here I am writing about it.

I make no apologies for being real. I'm warning you now; please don't expect this to be a book from the pastor. There may be some offensive language and/or terminology in my writing of this book. This is where I am today. This is what I am releasing. I'd rather release all of the garbage that I'm feeling today so that I can start my healing process tomorrow. I refuse to let the image of churchy people dictate my heart and feelings. I can't live for an image to please others. Today, I'm writing as a woman who is fighting for her sanity and her life.

There were almost 200 people on our guest list. At the time I am writing, only three people have called or texted me today to see how I was doing. I'm sure there are those who are praying and want to give me some space. However, it goes to show that when you are making plans and spending money for hundreds of people to come and celebrate your life event, in the grand scope of things, you truly only matter at the moment. I guess that when the wedding celebration was canceled, to some, it was a mere "to do" for the day, and they canceled that event and penciled in another event. But to me, it's a day that I'm fighting with everything within me to live and get through the night...

"Written December 2013"

GET THROUGH THE NIGHT

IT'S DECEMBER 21, 2013, AT 12:15 P.M., AND I'M A BALL of nerves. My hands are shaking, and my stomach is in knots. That is the usual reaction of a bride, I suppose. And anyone who knows me knows that when I put on an event, I'm a stickler about starting on time. The invitation stated that the ceremony starts at 12:30 p.m. The reason the ceremony had to start on time was because the reception was located about 30 minutes away from the church.

So with the bridal party, anticipating almost 200 guests, and the wedding program, it was important to start on time, so those who so graciously volunteered to help with this joyous occasion could leave immediately after the ceremony to help set up the reception site.

It's now 12:23 p.m., and my hands are shaking even more. I'm such a mess right now. Hair pulled to one side — just like the plan so that my one and only tattoo can show and be revealed to the world on this day. A beautiful rose in memory of my father (he had a red rose tattoo) and the initials of the man I so dearly love and gave my all to, along with my initials and our last name: R.C.K.C.W. That's how much I love this man. I was willing to endure emotional and physical pain to express my love. Love makes you do some crazy stuff... I really didn't want to say "stuff," but for the sake of being a lady, I'll leave it at that.

The playlist was carefully selected to reflect our love, our endurance, and our relationship. My cousin, an Indie Artist named Mista Youngblood from Southern California, was selected to be our guest soloist for this joyous occasion. Music was our thing. We would listen to music for hours and sing to each other and laugh. Even the favors were C.D.s of some of our favorite love songs. The label of the CD reads "R.C.K.C.W. THE PERFECT MIX 12.21.13" with 14 of the most beautiful songs.

But instead of the handpicked playlist playing, the bridesmaids lining up, the groomsmen adjusting their ties, the family and the guests gathering, at 12:30 p.m. on a beautiful sunny, crisp December afternoon I am sitting at my laptop listening to Chrisette Michelle, "Get Through the Night." There will be no marriage celebration today. At least not for me. How could I stand before almost 200 people and declare my love and happiness for being married to a man who for a year had disrespected me, treated me like I was just some woman he was dating, and within 60 days of being released from prison, had broken the marriage vows we took a year ago? I couldn't do it. I wanted to, but I couldn't.

I wanted the world to meet and know the man who made me laugh and made me smile. In retrospect, however, I realize he really charmed the hell out of me. Yep! I got played! He worked that good ole prison game, and like a damn fool, I fell for it. I guess that's what happens when you have a big heart and so much love to give, that when your heart is bursting at the seams to release love to someone, you fall prey and become vulnerable to see the best in a person. Even though they have time and time again shown that the best they can offer you is the life they've been living — a life of deception, manipulation, and lies.

You can see the best in a person, and you can want the best for that same person, but if they don't want more, you can't make them want a better life. If their only aspiration in life is to work the government system of Section 8, welfare, and defraud the medical system to get a "crazy" check, you can't make them want more. Did he really say to me he could get a check from social security by playing crazy just to get some type of temporary income until a real job came through? I understand and even appreciate the desire to be able to bring some type of income to the table, but isn't that illegal? Isn't that a lie? What type of lies would have to be told to the doctor to be deemed mentally disabled enough to collect the crazy check? And if you can play that role to lie to medical professionals to get a check, then I wondered how good of a liar are you to lie to me with a straight face?

It was the lies that got me... again. And not just the verbal lies but his eyes lied as well. Body language revealed when the lies were being told. The stuttering to get a story out revealed the lies. I thought I was the only one who read the lies in his eyes, but it turns out my son also saw it. He later revealed to me that he could tell something wasn't right. He said he just didn't look right. Something had changed, and he was different. It's sad that a person doesn't understand when you have a spiritual connection as strong as we had; when things are good, we feel it, and we know it. By the same token, when things are bad, we sense it, and we know it. When things are OFF and WRONG, we sense it and know that too. He only wanted to believe the connection worked when things were good. Well, I guess I shouldn't say that because when he was incarcerated on more than one occasion, he would sense the presence of a man around me, and when he called, he would question me about it, and he would be spot on! I found it funny how he was more in tune with me while he was locked up than he was when he came home.

It is now 1:04 p.m., and my will to live and face another day is resurfacing. Yes, it was bad over the past 48 hours. I didn't want to live. I'm surprised I'm still here. The thoughts that came to my mind over the past couple of days were surely supposed to take me out. There have been several pastors who have committed suicide over the past few months. And as I sat on my couch in the dark, drowsy from the sleeping pills and Amsterdam Peach Vodka, I said out loud, "I wonder if those pastors who committed suicide went to heaven." I considered how my life insurance was in place for my son and knew that he would be taken care of if I killed myself. I read the policy recently to know that it would still be effective even if I took myself out because the policy was more than two years old.

I wanted to die to escape the pain of the embarrassment of being taken advantage of, yet again, by this man. I didn't want to see December 21, 2013, because that day was supposed to be so special and full of love. I felt too ashamed to face all of the people I had convinced that he was a good person and a changed man. I felt so horrible for the friends who helped me and took on some of the expenses of the wedding celebration. They knew I was footing the bill by myself since he was recently home from prison and didn't have a job yet. They saw the stress and the pressure I was under and wanted to be a blessing. I crumbled under pressure.

I couldn't deal with his lies another day, and I canceled the wedding on November 16, 2013, at 2:30 a.m. after he sent me a text message telling me he couldn't come home until his daughter who had run away came back home. He was already staying away from home. He was staying about 30 miles away at the house of his step-daughter, who had custody of her siblings, including his two sons. He was supposed to be there to help them out.

When I tried to call him back to get clarity, he wouldn't answer his phone. What real man sends a text message of such importance to his wife at 2:15 a.m.? But that's how he communicates... via text. One would think that a man of 43 years would know that a text message isn't the best, neither the most efficient way to communicate important issues to anyone and especially your spouse. Why was that text a deal-breaker? Well, it wasn't JUST the text. There was already a lot of suspect behavior taking place, and the text message revealed that this man was lying to me once again.

I was tired of putting up with his lies and, at this point, pretending to everyone that I was still a happy woman. He was lying to me, and I was tired of it. Weeks later, he finally told me the truth in a three-part series. He would never just come right out and be honest. Every time we talked about it, he revealed a little more of the story. I told him that his phone indicated that he was out of town when I called him. He said he was at his kids' house when he sent me the text and then put the phone down and went to sleep. I responded to his text immediately because I happened to be awake. As a married woman who had become accustomed to her husband being home and in bed with her, once he left and started spending the night away from home "to be with his children," I stopped sleeping well at night. When I responded to his text, he didn't respond. When I called, I became furious. I could tell this lying fool was out of town!

The story was that he took his nephews to their granny's house in Sacramento. That would be considered out of town or out of the area from where he was. Then he said his kids' aunt, who had been hanging out and staying the night at the house with them, asked him to drive her to Sacramento to take her son's home. So, he drove this woman who was having marital issues (although he said she was happily married, she put it out there on Facebook that she was having issues during that time) to another family member's house who lived about an hour away and back. How cozy? How honorable and noble of this man?

The problem I had with that is when he's away "with his children," he ignores my calls and my texts. He's too busy to talk to his wife, see about his wife, or be concerned about his wife, but he can drive another woman and her sons to a city an hour away. The bad part about it is this woman, and her issues were so important that he would risk driving her this distance, knowing he didn't even have a driver's license. I guess some people were just worth the risk.

From his perspective and even some of his family members, he tried to say that I wasn't supportive of his children. Well, let's set the record straight. First of all, while he was locked up, I became close to his daughter, who lived out of state. Like him, she was a little charmer as well. She would reach out on Facebook to say hello and various pleasantries. I always knew the next request would be can I have, can I get, or can you send me? There were times I did help her out and sent her money. Then there were times when I wouldn't be able to because I had just sent him money for his books or had just sent him a package of food and toiletries. I made sure they had each other's addresses so she could write to him and he could write to her. In fact, during his entire jail/prison ordeal this last time (because there were a couple of stints before), I was the liaison and the bridge that connected him to his family. They weren't on good terms when he got arrested, and I was the one who helped them all to reconnect.

Sadly, his sons' mother died on January 1, 2013. I was with him in the visiting room at San Quentin when the officer came and told him the sad news. I was glad that I was there with him. Even though he was now my husband, I knew they had history, and her being the mother of his sons, I didn't want him to feel like he couldn't or shouldn't grieve her death. I know what it's like to have a parent die, and my heart went out to his children.

His family would call me and ask me what we were going to do about his sons, who were now in the custody of their older sister (his step-daughter). I had never even met his children and told them that he had to make that decision and that it would be something we would have to address when he came home. But they were persistent and saying they didn't want to go through the same thing they went through with the boys' mother.

Apparently, she didn't let his family see them very often. She often expressed a strong dislike for his mother. I don't know why they didn't have a good relationship, but I do know it was not good. I was told that the kid's mother was a very evil woman who manipulated and played games with him for years. I was told she used the children against him, and whenever they broke up, she would use the kids as bait to get him back, and it usually worked. This man loves his children a lot, I was told. But I didn't understand how a man who loved his children as much as they said he did couldn't keep his life on track enough to stay out of prison to be there for them. And if he loved him the way he said he did, he had a strange way of proving it.

When the kids' mother died, I knew things in our relationship were going to be different. We would have to make plans and provision for his sons. He had two young sons with this woman, and she had three daughters. He NEVER indicated to me that he felt a parental obligation to the daughters — not one time. It was always about getting his life together and back on track so that he could get custody of his sons, and we would raise the boys together. Again, NEVER did he express an obligation to the girls. But when he came home, a lot changed and all of a sudden, he felt an obligation to all five children instead of just his sons.

I don't have a problem with feeling an obligation to parent children who you watched grow up and were once a father figure in their lives. The problem I do have is that you say you are there for them when in reality, you are just another mouth for them to feed and for them to support. You see, they have an income, a place to live, and transportation. So, in reality, you are an adult figure in the house, but the real woman of the house is in control and is calling the shots.

Finally, he let me meet the kids. I was able to meet them all, except for the little woman of the house. He refused to let me meet the adult daughter. I have been within 20 feet of her when picking them up from the house, but he scurried me back to the car and said now is not the time to meet her.

Whenever he would call me from the house, if she came home, he would have to get off of the phone with me. The day I picked them up, and she was in the driveway, she snapped at him and gave him some type of instruction concerning the boys, and he said okay, but his body language and tone were very "mouse" like. I can't figure out for the life of me what the deal between the two of them could be. I'm not insinuating any type of inappropriate relationship, although others have questioned me and wondered if that was the case.

Later on, he did tell me how she dressed provocatively and tried to come on to him. I knew there was a reason he had to submit to this twenty-three-year-old. In reality, he had no control in that house, and to be honest, I couldn't see him staying there for too much longer. He's good at being in and out of people's lives. He's as temporary as they come. No roots. No substance. He'll pick up and go at the drop of a dime. He won't take an overnight bag, a toothbrush, or a jacket. This man is good at walking away with just the clothes on his back.

It is now 2:03 p.m., and my breathing is a little more normal. The ceremony would have been over by now. I guess pictures would be taken by now, and the guests would be smiling and talking about how beautiful the ceremony was. It was going to be really special too. I was looking forward to Mista Youngblood's performance of his song, "In Love with You." He is a natural-born performer. He would have rocked it. But it was the song at the reception that was going to send the ladies into a tizzy, "Don't Waste Time!" Now, that song is HAWT! Instead, here I sit with Chrisette on repeat.

I really thought her song, "A Couple of Forevers" was going to be the song that stayed in my head on this day. I certainly didn't see this coming. I had no idea the first time I heard this song that it would be my anthem for what was supposed to be my marriage celebration day. The "Willis Love Affair 2013" was the original theme for this day. It was supposed to be a day that represented love, endurance, and romance. I wanted this day to be a day where my husband was grandly presented to the world. I wanted this day to bless other couples and provide an environment for people who don't usually express their love publicly to feel safe to do so in the presence of other couples in love. I wanted my husband to have a day like he's never had before.

He's never been made a fuss over. He's never had a big party like this just for him. I wanted to show people how much I loved him by giving him a day he would remember for the rest of his life. The problem is I forgot that this day wasn't just about him. It was supposed to be a day that made me feel just as special. But I couldn't, and I didn't, because I was the one putting up all of the finances, doing all the work, and making all of the arrangements. The only thing he had to do was show up. I guess that's why it wasn't meant to be. Things were off. As a husband, he had much more responsibility than merely showing up. He didn't even have a ring for me. I bought every ring that represented our relationship. I bought the cubic zirconia ring, I bought our engraved wedding bands, and I bought my real diamond ring. It is now 2:17 p.m., and now I'm laughing and smiling. It's starting to make sense. The fog is clearing from last night.

People have been telling me God wants more for me and that I deserve more. It's hard to understand and even believe it when your heart is so wrapped up in caring for the needs of someone else. Even if I felt like I should have waited to marry him (and clearly, I should have), I still felt like it was already done, and I had an obligation to make it work. But I see that you can't make someone do better if they just aren't capable of doing so. My friends told me that I deserved better than what he was giving me. They would tell me how beautiful, smart, and intelligent I am, and that I could do better. The problem was that I felt like such an idiot for marrying this man after he had only shown me a history of lies and inconsistency. How can I be so smart and so stupid at the same time? And the funniest part about this whole ordeal is the people who said "I told you so" are the people you would least expect to say it.

It was his own family. His own flesh and blood were the ones who said behind my back, "It's not like we didn't tell her who she was marrying." Wow! I was even told directly by one of his sisters, "I supported you with who you chose to marry!" I was in such shock because she was referring to her own brother. But to his face, she smiles and says how much she loves him, that she is so thankful to have him back around, and that she is praying for him and his wife.

His family is really one of the reasons I ended up back in this tangled web of lies. I was there for him when they weren't. I mean that in the literal sense. Of the huge family he comes from, I was there when none of them would be, could be, or wanted to be. They were so thankful and appreciative of me loving and supporting their son and brother while he was in prison. Well, now I understand why! As long as I was there for him, they didn't feel the obligation to do so. It wasn't that they loved me or cared for me. They knew that I was a good woman and how much I loved him. They saw that I wouldn't abandon him. I kept my word to him. Any time I said I would be there or do something for him, I was there. They had made promises to him and had no condemnation about breaking those promises. And every time they didn't do what they told him they would do for him, I would have to make up for it.

If you've ever had a loved one in prison, you know how dependent they are on you. Your word means the world to them. If you said you were going to come to visit on a certain day, they are on pins and needles waiting for that day to come. If you say you will be sending them money or food packages, they are anxiously awaiting their name to be called to receive their commissary. Knowing that he had been in prison before and knowing how this whole process works, I couldn't understand how they were so careless about keeping their word or commitment. With their words, they expressed how much they loved him and were so excited for the bright future he had with me, but with their actions, he wasn't a priority.

I just had an "aha moment." My confusion about his words and actions has just been revealed. With words, he convinced me that he was a changed and different man, but his actions never did line up with his words. He's only doing what he knows to do. Whether a learned behavior in his family or something deeply embedded in his D.N.A., he knows to use words that sound good even if the actions never back up those charming words.

At 2:53 p.m., I just checked in online with Southwest Airlines for my flight tomorrow afternoon. It's funny because I didn't realize that our honeymoon flight was booked for literally 24 hours after the wedding ceremony. The flight is for 12:20 p.m. Since I paid for these tickets, I'm still taking the trip to San Diego. I deserve a break. It may not be a honeymoon trip, but I can still celebrate M.E. I've been through hell with this man, and I deserve a break for a couple of days to regroup. My neighbor told me that I needed to make the trip a rebirth experience. I agreed with him. I needed to get away and leave some things on the sands of San Diego to come back refreshed.

Just 48 hours ago, I didn't want to live. And 24 hours ago, I was planning NOT to live. I sent him text messages and told him that I wanted to die. I told him that I didn't want to live and face the embarrassment and shame of our relationship failing once again. I wasn't in a good place at all. I'm sure he saved the texts so he can show people how much of a mess I was at that time, which is why I don't have a problem writing about it. Hell, I figure if he will tell it, then let me tell it and get paid for it. So, if I haven't thanked you, I really appreciate your support in buying this book!

The fog and disbelief of my reality were crushing me. I couldn't believe after all of the months of planning and preparing for this day, that when it arrived, we wouldn't be celebrating our first anniversary with family and friends, but that divorce papers would be sitting on my kitchen table ready to be filed. How could this be? This was supposed to be a testimony of a great comeback from the depths of prison and despair to a life of prosperity and happiness. But the comeback wasn't what I thought it would be. I thought he was going to come back, on fire for God, and walk in his purpose as a man of God, a husband, and a father. Instead, he came back and went back to what was familiar and comfortable to him.

As I listen to the words of this song that has played probably 20 times already, I have more clarity. The Bible verse, "weeping may endure for a night, but joy comes in the morning" (Psalm 30:5b), is making more sense to me. I am sitting here in the middle of the day looking at clear blue skies outside of my window while I am having a nighttime experience. But once I get through this "night" experience, I will smile again. Everything will be different tomorrow. I just gotta get through the night as my girl keeps singing to me.

I can't help but go back to how I got here. I have to press the rewind button of my mind to think about what led up to this day of disappointment. We've always had a connection. Whether we were together or not, we seemed to stay connected and in tune with each other. I don't know if that is a good thing or one of those "soul ties" that need to be broken. At this point in my life and where I am today, I'm not feeling those churchy terms and jargon. I think we've ruined so many lives in the church by being biblically and doctrinally unsound for the sake of sounding profound and deep.

The best way I can describe it is a "connection." Even though things are all bad between us at this very moment, a place in my heart still recalls how special that connection we shared was. I wouldn't even be surprised at this very moment if he were thinking of me. I'm almost sure he's tried to text me or call me today, but I've blocked him from my phone. There's no need to talk to him today. He's there, and I'm here. If I meant anything at all to him, he would be right here by my side, and I wouldn't be writing at this time. But again, I realize he's not capable of loving me the way I need to be loved, and so here I sit alone at 3:47 p.m. of what was supposed to be our special day.

Back in August of 2010, after three months of our last break up, I received a text from the girlfriend of a friend of his. The text stated who she was and that she was informing me that he had been arrested and was about to be transferred to North County. I was in shock! I received the text while I was at the hair salon, and all I could do was sit in the chair, stunned. I texted back and told her that he had been on my mind and that I felt like something was wrong with him, but I had no way of contacting him. I'm sure she didn't care about my feeling or inclinations concerning him. She was just delivering a message.

But I had to express to someone that we still had a connection, and, in my heart, I felt like something was wrong with him. She told me that he was going to be calling me later. I had no idea how that was going to work, but I just had to wait to hear from him.

Sure enough, a day or two later, he called. When I told him that I felt like something was wrong, he was extremely happy to hear that we were still connected, and more importantly, that I still cared. If he ever needed me to care for him, it was now. I didn't forget how and why we had broken up yet again, so while I was glad to hear his voice and to know he was alive, part of me felt like, "this is what you get for leaving me… again."

Within a few moments of the conversation, I asked him if he wanted me to call his mother to tell her where he was and his situation. He reluctantly said yes. Immediately, the first of what felt like hundreds of requests over the three years began.

He asked me if I could send him a few dollars. I had no idea how to send money to someone in jail. He only had so much time, so he was trying to explain it to me and trying to tell me about a website to go to that would guide me on how to send it. Again, I was so unfamiliar with this process that I could barely understand what he was saying to me. I was in the car when he called me so I wrote as much of the information down that I could, including his state-issued identification number, the address to the jail, and whatever other information he was spitting out that would help get the $20 I was planning to send him. I jotted down the information, and he told me he would be calling me back. At this time, I wasn't paying for his calls. He had a friend who was also in jail who had put a lot of money on a prepaid card, and he would call his girlfriend, and the girlfriend would call me for him. Again, this whole situation was new to me, and all I knew was the man I once loved and had planned to marry was in jail and was calling me through a friend's girlfriend.

I was angry with him for leaving me. I was angry with him for knowing that I was good to him, yet he still walked away and went back to his kids' mother, and they still didn't stay together. I knew that his life with me was better than without me, and I had a feeling he would end up back in jail. But when it actually happened, my heart went out to him. I will never forget that day we talked, and I told him I would call his mother. I was in the parking lot of Southland mall. I called her to tell her that he had been arrested and was in jail. Her response was, "That is my son, and all I can do is pray for him." Then she told me she had to go and abruptly hung up the phone.

I literally stood in that parking lot starring at the phone with my mouth wide open! I couldn't believe it! This is your son. Your OLDEST son and yes, he's been in trouble before, but he's in jail now, and that's all you have to say is you will pray for him! She didn't ask if he needed anything. She said she had to go and hung up the phone. I was so messed up that I called his brother-in-law and told him what just happened. I told him that I felt like I'd done something wrong and perhaps offended his mother by calling her to tell her about him being in jail. I asked his brother-in-law what I should do. He told me to follow my heart, and if I wanted to help him, to be there for him. The angry black woman in me said to ignore him and let him suffer, but my heart was so broken that his mother basically turned her back on him that I felt like the least I could do was be a friend and be there for him.

When he called back, I made sure I got the information so that I could send him the few dollars he asked for to help him through this ordeal that he thought was going to be a 45-day journey. Based on the crime, he was being told by other offenders in jail that he should only get about 45 days. I figured I would be a friend and be supportive of him being down 45 days. He asked for my address because he wanted to write to me to share some things that were on his heart and express his "undying love" for me. Well, of course, you love me NOW! You need me, is what I was thinking.

Yes, he did need me. What type of person would I be to leave him in such a situation? I couldn't in good conscious abandon him in such a serious time of need. Although I'd never had the experience of loving someone in jail who didn't have anyone else to come to his aid, I felt like the way you show someone you love them, even as a friend, was to be there for them in a real way. So, in the beginning, I set out to be his friend. I just wanted to be a friend, and that was my only intention.

Well, it is now 6:30 p.m. and the reception for the Willis Love Affair 2013 would have been winding down. By now, we should have been in joyful bliss and exhaustion from dancing with family and friends for hours. The D.J. we were to hire had been sent an awesome playlist that incorporated some of the most fun party songs from the '80s and the '90s. It was going to be a prom, birthday celebration, and wedding reception all in one! The fun we were supposed to have on this day would have been so memorable. Instead, I just spent the last hour sifting through letters he wrote to me from county jail and prison. He's been calling me Mrs. Willis for years, even before we were married. That man just knew I was going to be his wife. He always said you have to claim it and speak it into the atmosphere! I wonder why in the hell he couldn't speak right, do right, and honor this marriage into the atmosphere!

I just changed the music. After five hours of "Get Through the Night" on repeat, I change the song to "Ten Foot Stilettos." Chrisette is one bad chick! Now she's telling me how to stand free and tall above the drama and walk it off in ten-foot stilettos! This will be on repeat for a while.

Back to these county letters — even as I read them, I feel the heart and sincerity of a man who truly wanted to do better and be better. Sometimes people who are incarcerated play games with people on the outside with no intention of doing better. They talk a good game to get what they need while they are locked down. A friend of mine helped me to understand that when a person is incarcerated, all they have is time, and it's easier for them to stay focused in a confined environment. So, everything they say and intend to do can truly be from the heart.

The challenge comes when they have the freedom and the choice to do otherwise. In his case, I guess that's what happened. Perhaps he did have the most honorable and best intentions, but when reality set in, we clearly saw that he chose otherwise.

When we first started communicating via letters while he was in county jail, I would let him have it! Everything I wanted to say to him about our breakup, I said it. I figured while he was trapped and stuck in jail, I could just vent and release and tell him EXACTLY how I felt. Since I'm being there for him and providing him with financial support, the least he could do in return was hear me out. It was really weird for me in the beginning to write him letters in jail. I was used to talking to him on the phone or in-person, so my letters were very intense because I wanted to get a point across and I would often feel like I had to get it all out in one letter because I didn't know if I'd ever get the chance again.

I would write one long letter after another to tell him how much he hurt me and how much I trusted him to do the right thing *this* time. I didn't know how he would receive what I had to say, but at least I was getting it off my chest. He needed to know how much I loved him, sacrificed for him, and supported him. I wanted him to know how angry I was at him for walking away as if I was nothing to him. He needed to know that I was hurt, and I was pissed off.

Being a writer, I realize that it was his letters that captured my heart. I am a lover of written words, especially handwritten words. I identify handwritten words as an extension of the heart because that's how I feel. When I write, it's an expression of my heart being conveyed on paper. I assumed it was the same from him. His words stimulated my mind and my soul. I got caught up in his letters. He would pour out his heart to me in those letters, and I would respond with anything and everything I needed to say.

North County Jail, located at 5555 Giant Highway in Richmond, CA, was the first leg of this journey. This is the address I started receiving letters from and sending letters to. Sometimes I would handwrite his letters. Other times, I would type them. Here is a copy of an actual letter I sent him. This is a glimpse into my mindset at that time on that date. As hard as it is to read those words today, knowing how things changed, it's a harsh reality. I should have stuck to my guns. I should have stood firm. However, I chose otherwise. (Actual letter: written September 6, 2010)

Dear Mr. Willis,

I hope this letter finds you well. I just received your last letter, and I'm like whoooaaaa... hold on, dear heart!

It's already been established time and time again, I love you and never stopped. You say your love for me has never stopped. I can only speak from what I know to be real and my actions that have backed it up.

I'm still listening to you and reading your letters with all of the thoughts of your actions toward me. And with that I want you to know I can't even discuss marriage to you right now… for more than one reason. The first being that little issue of finalizing your divorce. And secondly, because you aren't able to show me that things are different at this time. I would be a damn fool to get sucked back into thinking this time the words are different. Yes, I will admit… I'm damaged! I'm damaged badly and probably have a little hardness in my heart that not only are you getting but other men who are approaching me these days. I'm so OVER words, not just from you but from all men. You know my motto, you can show me better than you can tell me, and until you show me, I'm not falling for anything.

It trips me out that a year almost to the day you left me while I was in Atlanta you end up in jail. That's a trip! Then we got back together and you paint the room at the church, I pay you, you kiss me and say "I love you" and leave and say you'll be back in an hour and that was the LAST TIME I saw you. Then we try to be cordial and stay in touch after a series of texts and phone fights and I reach out to you and tell you how much I was hurting and needed to talk to you. You call me back, talk to me for a few minutes, and hang up on me... why? Because of the other woman who walked up (I don't know if it was Felicia, Angela or whomever).

THEN you promise to send flowers to my job and don't do it and THEN you text me while you are out partying with 20-something-year-old females having "the time of your life" and spending "way too much money" and then say you were coming over when you left the club and NEVER showed up.

Then all of a sudden, I get the phone call that you're in jail. (Once again, where are all the other females now? Where is Felicia now? She can get you to drop everything based on a lie about your children whenever she wants you back but she can't be there for you now? Or, is she actually there for you and I'm just in addition to whatever she's doing? Who knows? ...but the truth always gets exposed).

Nevertheless, here I am being a "friend" to you. Showing you better than I could tell you what a TRUE friend is supposed to be. But please don't get it twisted. You are not playing me, and you are not getting over on me and you are NOT using me. I wanted to be here for you. My heart goes out to the man I know you are supposed to be. Not the trickster, the deceiver, and manipulator you have been to me throughout our relationship.

I don't fall for syrupy sentimentalism. That doesn't work on me anymore, Roy. That's B.S. that you can use on someone else. You told Felicia's daughter that Felicia was the only woman you ever really loved (remember that?). Now you're telling me the same thing. I deserve better than that, Roy. I at least deserve to be told the truth. Please stop lying to me. Please stop telling me you want to marry me. Please stop saying God said we were going to be husband and wife. I say that because He hasn't spoken that to me. I believed it with all my heart back then but now I'm not so sure.

I would like to believe it now but that's not what I'm getting from God. I've asked God. I've prayed and He's not telling me that. He's silent on the matter... I wish He would just say YES or NO, but I get nothing at this time. And until then, I just ask that you don't even mention marriage to me. That's not something to play with in my eyes. I wanted to be your wife. Now I can't imagine that role. I just can't. I don't have clarity about being Mrs. Willis anymore. God is going to have to really speak LOUD AND CLEAR to me about that. But again, for now... nothing!

I know it seems like I'm mad but I'm not. I just need you to understand where I'm coming from. I love you but you are not going to talk your way back in my life again. Like you said in your first letter, you are going to have to fight and put in a hell of a lot of work if you even think you want me. And trust me, it's not going to be easy. Don't you know how much I sacrificed for you? I'm not even talking about money. I'm talking about my name, my character, my reputation, my family... so much, all because I LOVE YOU, R.O.Y.! But you didn't show me the same commitment, neither loyalty. Your family loves me, but they've had some negative things to say about me for loving you and being there for you by letting you stay with me. I'm no fool! I've lost friends and associates because of my relationship with you.

Like I said, I'm here for you as much as I can be and when I'm able to. I don't want you to get it twisted into thinking I'm expecting anything more from you.

So please, please, please respect my wishes and do not mention marriage again... please... that discussion only needs to happen after you get out, after you are divorced, after you are working again and after you have a ring to propose to me... until then... we don't even need to go there.

Again, I am not mad... I just really need you to understand where I'm coming from."

Now that I read my own letters from three years ago, I say to myself, "I told you so." Here it is in black and white. The lines in the sand were drawn. The boundaries were set. But I accepted more of his letters — more of his words. And with that... I got caught up. I was on the hook and believed that things would be different this time. How foolish of me. The man had so much potential, and I thought because he got arrested and was in jail at the age of forty, this had to be the last time. I thought he would truly change his life based on this experience.

I chose to stay involved and be a friend. Again, I vented and told him exactly how I felt about his treatment of me and was cautiously proceeding with letting him into my life. I was there because no one else was there for him. I started with sending him that first twenty dollars, and then he continued to tell me how he had nothing in there and needed a few things to get by. I didn't realize how limited things were in jail. I didn't know you didn't have even the basics like paper, pen, envelopes, and stamps to even reach out to your loved ones. And if you didn't have money for commissary, you were stuck with the slop they served during "chow."

The more he shared with me the conditions of jail, the more

I felt sorry for him. After all, this is a man I loved, and although we weren't together, I didn't have it in my heart to turn my back on him as he lived in a cage with all types of other criminals and was experiencing all types of mental and emotional anguish. I know he got himself in that situation. But "what would Jesus do?" I felt compelled to be there for him. I knew it was a risk, but I honestly felt like it was the right thing to do. Even Jesus said when you feed, clothe, visit someone in prison, we are doing it to Him. I felt like I was doing the will of the Lord by helping Roy while he was in prison.

In retrospect, Jesus said to feed, clothe, and visit, He never said anything about getting into a relationship and getting married. That's where ministry ended, and my own desires stepped in.

ABANDONMENT

IT WAS THE MARRIAGE TO ROY THAT REALLY MADE THE feelings of abandonment resurface. I had done so much for him while he was in prison that I believed his love for me would cause him to reciprocate the same loyalty. It wasn't like that at all. He didn't value or appreciate the years of sacrifice I went through for him. There were times I went without to make sure he had commissary. I had to keep money on the phone so that he could call me whenever he needed to. By the time we were married, I had given up so much to help him through a tough time.

Not only did I make financial sacrifices, but my name and reputation were also scrutinized for marrying him, especially while he was in prison. How could a pastor marry a prisoner? People supported me, but I know there were a lot of whispers behind my back. The only recourse in this situation was that he came from a family of pastors, evangelists, and ministers. Since he was known to be their family member, people thought perhaps things could work out between us with God's help. I guess that's what I was hoping as well, but the miracle I hoped for just didn't happen.

As we went through the ups and downs in our marriage, I began to see my insecurities spill over in other areas of my life. After supporting him for the majority of his four years in prison, he left me to go be with his children and stepchildren. I felt like the outsider and the other woman all over again. Although we were still married, he went back to live in the same house he used to when he was still with his kid's mother. I was his wife. I was his support system. I was there for him when nobody else was there, but he made a decision to walk away, showing me that I wasn't as important to him as I thought.

Since I was still pastoring, I had the church to focus on while he was gone. It wasn't easy, but I had to do it. I had to continue to be the pastor, minister, and leader in a fellowship we supported and evangelized as speaking engagements came up. During this time, some people decided to leave the ministry for various reasons. When you pastor a church or lead a ministry, it's inevitable that people will come and go. That's just part of the calling.

You have to realize that people come to you, and you are assigned to teach them whatever God gives you for them at that particular time in their life. You give as much as you can to them in terms of advice, wise counsel, guidance, and information, and all you want in return is to see them blessed, and their lives blossom and purpose be fulfilled. The hard part is that sometimes, you don't get a chance to see those things. They may leave before then, and you may feel it's not time for them to leave your ministry, but you have to let them go. It's painful. It hurts, and sometimes it can leave you wondering if you did something wrong or if you could have done some different or better to make them stay.

Sometimes you are happy to see some people leave because all of the hell they raised at the church. There are others that you just don't want to see them leave. Those are the times you have to rely on God's wisdom and know that He already knew their beginning and end time in your ministry. That's the spiritual side. However, it doesn't always soothe the natural side. It can leave you broken even though you don't show it.

I have to be honest, feelings of rejection were present during the time I pastored because I felt like I've done all I could to help a person or a family, and they walk away like it's nothing. It isn't about ego. As I said, these are very real issues that happen in church. If a pastor has unresolved issues from their past, these are the types of situations that will make them question their call. Sadly, it will also make them act out in negative ways. If you've ever heard of a pastor talking badly about someone because they chose to leave their church, chances are they have some unresolved abandonment issues that are surfacing.

Perhaps you've heard of a pastor speaking curses over

people and saying they won't prosper, or they will lose their job or even die because they left their church when God hadn't told them to leave. More than likely, that pastor has some unresolved issues of rejection they are dealing with.

We see the spiritual gift that pastors have, but we often forget the human side and that they are just as fragile as anyone else. Sure, they can be gifted to preach and can be very charismatic, but underneath all of that, there is a real person who struggles with insecurities at times. I'm speaking from experience. I'm speaking from the other side.

I know what it's like to preach to hundreds of people at a time and watch God bless them tremendously to the point of crying and falling out at the altar. I know what it's like to have the accolades and praises because of how I preached. I know what it's like to speak a word into someone's life before it comes to pass and to be thanked and honored for allowing God to use me to be a blessing. I also know what it means to go home alone after great church services and cry myself to sleep.

There were many times I cried because I wanted the blessings that I watched other people get after I prayed for them or preached to them. I cried because after preaching a house down, I couldn't afford to go out to dinner to eat like everyone else, and I had to go home and cook a simple meal for my son and myself. I know what it's like to stand on a platform and feel great and then go home and feel empty.

There were plenty of times I felt like I was fulfilling the call of my life, while living an unfulfilled life. Some issues were buried deep within that I never addressed. I didn't know it at the time, but I was a ticking time bomb.

DADDY ISSUES

Dear Daddy,

Today, while riding down Highway 99 returning home from Sacramento, tears began to roll down my face. I tried to be a big girl and not cry but the more I wiped them away the more they fell. Today would have been your seventieth birthday. Although this was supposed to be your day of celebration, I wanted the gift. I wanted the gift of your touch. I wanted the gift of your hug. I just wanted my Daddy.

There is so much I've needed to say to you since you left me when I was only nine years old. Although you've been gone for forty years, you are never forgotten. Some days my heart aches because of the love I have for you and I just want to know if you would love me the same. I wonder if you would be proud of me through my flaws and failures. I wonder if my mistakes would have ruined our relationship or caused us to grow closer. I struggle with wondering if you would see me as good enough.

Daddy, I know you had your own struggles. I know you had your demons to fight but sometimes I can't help but feel abandoned. Daddy, you left me. I needed you. I had so many questions throughout forty years of life without you. Mom did a great job, but I still needed my Daddy to get the male perspective. I needed guidance and direction from someone who didn't want anything from me and who had my best interests at heart. I needed the help of a man who didn't have an ulterior motive.

I'll never know what it means to be a Daddy's girl. I've come to accept it. I never allowed another man to take your place. When you left me, I learned to live my life with a hole in my heart that could never be filled. I have loving uncles and have had some male mentors during my life, but nobody could ever fill the void of you. I've always reserved a place in my heart for you.

So, on this day, February 8, 2020, I say to you, happy birthday, Daddy. I miss you like crazy and through my tears, I celebrate your memory.

I love you with all my heart, your baby girl.

MY DADDY DIED WHEN I WAS NINE YEARS OLD. I STILL remember that devastating day. It was a Sunday morning. My oldest brother and I were at my grandmother's house. Mom was at work, so we stayed with Granny so that we could go to church with her. We were watching Popeye on television. All of a sudden, Mom walked into Granny's house with her brother, our Uncle Wayne, turned off the television. She knelt down and hugged us both. Through tears, she said, "your father died." We started crying. In my nine-year-old mind, I still didn't understand. I still didn't grasp the fact that the man I barely knew, I barely saw, and I barely understood had died. All I knew was a sadness that overtook me that would follow me for years to come.

As far as I remember, my father's funeral was the first funeral I attended. We went shopping to buy new clothes for this occasion. I didn't understand it, but that's what the family did for us. People gave us extra hugs and attention. As adults, I'm sure they've experienced the death of a loved one before, so perhaps they were giving us as much love as possible to help us deal with the days to come.

We drove from the Bay Area to Fresno, where my father lived and died. I think he actually died in the city of Corcoran, where his parents and siblings lived, but his home was Fresno.

We stayed with my mother's childhood friend Brenda. I remember talking to one of my uncles a night or two before the funeral, and he told me about the injuries my father sustained in the "accident." He said his chest was crushed and his skull was cracked. I'm sure he said some other things, but that's what I remembered the most. I remember telling my mother what my uncle told me about my father's injuries, and she was upset. As a mother, I can see why she would be upset that an adult would tell a nine-year-old such gruesome details. I didn't need to know all of that. However, knowing me, I probably did ask, and he told me.

Knowing the details of his injuries didn't ease the pain of my loss. It only made me more curious. What could have possibly happened? We were told that he fell asleep driving his pickup truck, and he drove into a ditch. That's what we were told. Later on in life, other details were revealed that he was unhappy and was actually drunk at the time of the "accident." Secrets began to be told, and some even said that he drove himself into the ditch. Plainly put, some said he committed suicide.

I wasn't there, so I have no idea what actually happened that day. What I do know is that for years the feeling of abandonment hovered over me. I always felt like my Daddy left me. I didn't feel like he was taken from me. I didn't feel like it was just an accident. I felt like he made a decision to leave me, and it hurt me to my core. I was angry with him. I mourned him year after year, but I was hurt and angry. I was angry that he missed so many important days in my life while growing up. He wasn't there for birthdays, proms, and graduations. I couldn't pick up the phone and call him when I needed advice from a man.

There were times in my teenage years when I was rebellious, and my mother would say, "If your father was still alive, you wouldn't be acting like this!" I would almost hate her for saying such a thing. In my mind, I would say, *well, he ain't here!* But because I have a Black Mama, I knew better than to backtalk, so instead, warm angry tears would just roll down my face. My tears and my glares at her would speak the words I couldn't dare utter to her. My tears and glares said *how dare you say such a painful thing?* I would have loved to have my Daddy around to correct me and stop me from making some of the mistakes I made in my life.

There were times I even blamed him! He was supposed to be there to stop me from falling for the slick words and tricks of some of the men who came into my life who took advantage of me. If he hadn't left me, I probably wouldn't have suffered so much. My abandonment was mixed with so many emotions: pain, anger, sorrow, despair, and fear. I loved my Daddy so much. He was so handsome. He was so strong. He was big and tall with a light complexion and good hair. He was fine. But in my mind, he chose to leave me. I thought he was strong, but maybe he wasn't as strong as he appeared to be. Was he really a weak man? Not weak in stature, but mentally and emotionally weak. If the whispers and secrets were true, did he cop-out? To this day, I don't have clear answers about the demons that fought my father. All I know is that he left me when I was nine years old. That void in my heart has never been filled.

Growing up, I was always mature for my age. I looked older, I carried myself older, and my body definitely developed fast. People always thought I was a grown woman, even though I was just a kid. I grew up in a strict Apostolic holiness church. The women didn't wear pants or makeup. The outward sign that you were saved was whether or not you wore pants. At a young age, I accepted the Lord Jesus Christ as my savior. I was filled with the Holy Ghost with the evidence of speaking in other tongues as the Spirit gave utterance. To some, that sounds weird, spooky, and even scary, but that was the teaching I grew up in. Later in life, I came to understand that the gift of tongues or praying in that heavenly language is actually a beautiful thing and less about the acceptance or appearance of spirituality by another person but rather a loving, caring relationship and conversation with God.

Back in those days, we weren't taught like that. If the "fire" of the Holy Ghost fell on you, then the first thing you did was come out of those pants! Throw them away. Burn them. Or, be as creative as one of my aunts and use your sewing skills to make those pants into a skirt! Yes, that's how they did it back in the '80s. Throughout my junior high and high school years, I was known as the girl who didn't wear pants. It made no sense to the other kids. To be perfectly honest, it didn't even make sense to me. I would just tell people it's because of my religion. Some people didn't celebrate holidays because of their religion; I couldn't wear pants because of my religion. It was embarrassing that I always stood out from the other kids my age. In order to feel better about myself, I had to dress as if I were confident about my looks. I started wearing heels to school. There were many times I was mistaken for one of the teachers. I wasn't only mistaken as a teacher by the students, but some of the male teachers as well. There were a lot of double-takes or longer-than-normal glares that the male teachers gave me.

I was beginning to notice how older men were attracted to me. Although I was a skirt-wearing church girl, I became aware of my womanhood and sexuality very early on. Again, I was forced to grow up faster because of my religion, and frankly, the boys weren't paying attention to me. But the men always gave me attention. The attention that I enjoyed. The attention that I craved.

I was still in high school when I had my first affair with a married man. I didn't know he was married at the time. I met him at a church convention of all places. He worked at the hotel that we stayed in. I think he was a security guard. He didn't wear the type of uniform with a badge, he wore a suit, and he would sit at a desk in one of the corridors where there wasn't a lot of traffic. My friends and I were wandering around the hotel, and we came across him. We caught eyes. I had become accustomed to that look; I knew he was interested. The next day we ran into each other at one of the restaurants. I think I was grabbing a breakfast bagel, and maybe he was getting coffee or something. He made small talk and told me to swing back by his station when I got a chance. I was interested, and so I told him I would.

Later on, I snuck away from my friends and made my way to him. We chatted for a while, and honestly, I don't remember what we talked about. As I recall, he was thirty-four, and I was sixteen. I graduated from high school at the age of seventeen. (I was a smart kid, so I skipped fifth grade.) This was the summer before school started, and I was entering my senior year. At his age, I don't know what he found appealing about me other than my curves. I wasn't overweight, but I wasn't small. I was a curvy sixteen-year-old with the body of a twenty-one-year-old, and clearly, he wanted me.

I walked with him on his rounds to make sure the area of the hotel he was responsible for was secure. There were small conference rooms along the way. He pulled me into one of the conference rooms, and we kissed. It was slow and passionate, and I thoroughly enjoyed it. He kissed me as if I were special, and he held me like I meant something to him. He pulled at my dress and noticed I had on stockings and a panty girdle. I know that is foreign to some people these days, but this was before the days of Spanx. I also had on a full slip — another undergarment that seems to have disappeared from most women's wardrobes.

When he noticed all of the barriers by slipping his hand under my dress, of course, he told me to come back tomorrow but not to wear the stockings. I leaned into his arms and rested my head on his chest and whispered, "Ok." As we walked back,

MISERY IN MINISTRY

I held his hand until we got closer to public view. I noticed he was wearing a gold band and pulled at it and asked if he was married. He said, "no" and that it was just a ring. With my silly young self, I believed him.

I met him the next day, minus the extra undergarments as instructed. Within a few minutes, we were walking on one of his rounds. He had a friend to relieve him at the desk. Again, he found a conference room for us, and we went in. I thought it was going to be another passionate kiss, but it wasn't. He went right for it. We had sex. It was quick and easy. Thankfully, he brought a condom and put it on. When it was over, he put it in the drawer of the desk we had just had sex on. I didn't feel anything. It wasn't good or bad. It was just done. I felt like he got what he needed, and that was it.

After the convention was over, we stayed in touch by phone and writing letters. This was before texts and emails, so I was excited to receive his handwritten letters in the mail. He wrote to me a couple of times; I kept his letters in a drawer in my bedroom. One day, for some reason, my mother went into my drawer and found the letter. It was all bad. She picked me up from school after play rehearsal and went absolutely off on me! I'm pretty sure I lied and told her we didn't do anything. All I know is she called him, and whatever she said to him, I never spoke to him or heard from him again.

About a month later, I was visiting my aunt and uncle. I was sitting on the couch with my uncle and looked at the gold band on his hand. Instinctively, I took him by the hand and asked him if I could see his ring. I don't know why, but I did. He took it off for me to see, and low and behold it was engraved! My heart sank. That's when I knew the guy was actually married. He didn't want me to take his ring off because it was probably engraved. That was the first lesson I learned as a girl about the tricks of a man.

Dating older men became a part of me. Most of the "boys" just didn't keep my interest. However, there was one boy in high school that I absolutely loved. We actually connected in junior high, but we ended up going to different high schools. Our birthdays were in the same month, but he was a year older. Since I skipped the fifth grade, most of my friends were at least a year older than me. He was my first experience with "love." We used to tell each other that we loved each other. He was a friend, but he had to be a secret. My religion wouldn't allow me to have a boyfriend and especially since he didn't go to church. He wasn't a bad guy at all. He just wasn't "saved."

I loved him. My heart was so connected to him, but I couldn't have a normal relationship with him because of church. Even after graduation, we stayed in touch. We were friends and lovers. We had a sexual relationship for a few years. When I met my son's father, and we started getting serious, I remember driving down the street and saying to myself, "But what about *him*?" We were no longer in a relationship, but he was my friend, and he had my heart. It was hard to imagine my life without him.

I told him about my new relationship, and he told me that I

should go ahead and pursue it. He said he would always love me, but I should move on. Although we didn't end on a bad note, it was painful to disconnect my heart from him. I had grown used to loving him. I didn't want to ever stop loving him. I had to learn to live my life without him being a part of it. It was a familiar type of pain. I wasn't ready to stop loving my Daddy, but I had to learn to love him in my heart but live without him the rest of my life.

My son's father, my first husband, Mr. Thornton LaCelle Davis, was eleven years older than me. Yep, another older man who spotted me and pursued me. I was visiting my mother, and he was visiting his friend, who was our next-door neighbor. I hadn't lived with my mother for over a year, so I never saw him. Apparently, he had seen me leaving her house before. This time, he made sure to stop me. He approached me, very nervously, and asked my name. I told him my name and asked his. He said his name was Pepe. I was like, can I please have your REAL name! He proudly said, "My name is Thornton LaCelle Davis."

We exchanged numbers and began dating. Although I was only twenty at the time, he was impressed with my maturity. He liked that I listened to smooth jazz and that I wasn't one of the wild, crazy girls. We dated for a few years, we traveled together, and we started planning our wedding. While planning our wedding, I found out that I was pregnant. The wedding was put on hold while I had our son, Jonathan LaCelle Davis. People assumed I automatically named my son after my oldest brother, but the truth is his father had an uncle named Jonathan as well. So, our son is blessed to carry the name from both sides of the family.

We ended up having a big wedding when Jonathan was nine months old. I'll never forget how that day ended up being one of the hottest days of the year. Just as I was about to enter the church, Jonathan was crying for me and threw up all over his little tuxedo we bought him for the wedding. My cousin was holding him and told me to go ahead and get to the altar and that he would take care of him. It was a beautiful day, and we had a lot of fun.

Our actual marriage was rocky. We had some hard times. I loved him. My love for him made me stay longer than I should have, but I didn't want my son to grow up without his father as I had. I tried. He had his own demons to fight. Things just didn't work out, and he moved out of California to Maine for a fresh start.

He moved when Jonathan was seven. I never saw him again. Jonathan visited him a few times in Maine. He had a set of twins. I was thankful that my son had siblings because I didn't want any more children. I always made sure my son kept in touch with his father. I never wanted them to be estranged. It was important to me that he knew his father. When he was younger, I would make sure he called his father once a week on his cell phone. I didn't have to speak to him, but I made sure Jonathan did. There were times we did speak when I wanted to give him updates about his son during his teenage years. Once

MISERY IN MINISTRY

he became an adult, I stepped back and didn't feel the need to talk to him.

On December 4, 2019, I received a text at 6:49 a.m., "I need you to call me. Urgent." The text came from LaCelle's mother. I was on my way to work and had just gotten on the BART. My brother and I had been chatting on the train when I looked down at my phone. Knowing that this was an odd text, I called her immediately, and all I could hear was muffled crying. We hurried off the train as I knew it was something bad, but I couldn't make out what she was saying. The call dropped. My phone rang again, and it was her husband. He said, "Kecia, Pep has passed..." I lost it right on the train platform, and thankfully, my brother Patrick was with me because I would have hit the ground. He held me up as I cried while trying to ask questions. Sam told me that they didn't have much information at the time and that they were trying to reach Jonathan, but they had an old number.

I had just got back from a cruise a couple of days earlier. When I left the house that morning, I didn't know if Jonathan was at home or at a friend's. We got on the train going back towards home (thankfully, we were only a couple of stations away). I called my husband to tell him the sad news. I asked him to knock on Jon's door to see if he was home. He said that he was home, and I told him not to say anything, and I would be home shortly. I was devastated. All I kept saying was, "My baby... oh God, how am I going to tell my baby!" The pain of the day, I found out about my own father's death hit me. Only this time, I was my mom, and Jonathan was me.

I don't remember if I called Mom or if Patrick called her. Everything at that moment was such a blur because I was just trying to get home to my son. By the time we pulled up to my house, our mom and oldest brother Jonathan was there. They came inside. I went to Jon's door and knocked. He answered, and I told him that I needed to talk to him. He opened the door and asked, "What, Mom?" He knew it was bad. "What, Mom? What is it?" All I could say was, "I'm so sorry, baby... your dad died." He let out a sound of agony that still pierces my heart to this day. He cursed. He screamed. He pounded his fist. And then he balled his eyes out.

His dad had his issues, but I taught Jonathan how to pray for his father since he was a little boy. I always wanted his dad to be okay because Jonathan would be okay. Jonathan was an adult when his dad passed, but it doesn't take away the pain of his loss. His loss and his pain are my pain as well. I hurt for my son. I hurt for LaCelle's parents and his family. Thankfully, I have a wonderful relationship with them, and they consider me their daughter, and they are my MiMi and Poppi. As a family, we keep each other encouraged.

LaCelle's remains were returned to his parents here in California. They put his remains in a beautiful blue marble urn. I met them at their house the day after it arrived. I carried it up the stairs. The funeral home in Maine left some of his remains in a small plastic envelope so that we could put them in keepsakes. I put some of his ashes in a keepsake for Jonathan.

The three of us sat in the living room and transferred the ashes. It was a little awkward, and we definitely had some shaky hands, but it had to be done. There was some laughter and at times, a tear or two, but we managed. At one point, I was left alone in the room with the urn; I prayed, thanked him for our son, and told him that I loved him. Being a minister, I went ahead and prayed the prayer of committal. I never imagined that my life, my calling, and my purpose would lead me to commit the father of my child back to God.

SANITY OVER ACCOLADES

"Pastor Kecia C. Taylor is known as a powerful preacher, a teacher with a sense of humor and a counselor with a compassionate ear," reads the first line of my ministry biography. Over the twenty-something years of ministry, I've heard the word "powerful preacher" more times than I could count. When you have a natural gift of gab, a natural inclination to connect with people, and a charismatic delivery, people will label you as "powerful." You have to show some level of ability to break down the word of God so that it can be applicable to everyday life.

However, I've noticed over time that if you haven't really studied as much as you should, you can get away with throwing your voice in such a way to sound convincing. Sprinkle in a few churchy terms like "God is good" and "God is going to bless you" here and there, and people will walk away from a church service and call you "powerful." It's sad to say it, but if you are a charismatic preacher, you can get away with a lot to have the people in an uproar of excitement if you don't put in the studying like you are supposed to.

I've seen it so many times where preachers would get up and "ride the wave." If the service was already on a high note from the worship or the choir singing, they would let the musicians "keep the party going" and just "shout the people" with some words of affirmation or encouragement and never open their Bible. Sometimes when I would see it, I would say to myself, *they didn't study* and laugh on the inside.

It has never been my intent to shortchange anyone when I delivered the word of God. When I studied, I would focus on the word God was giving me to deliver and pray that it would help someone who was in the service. I tried to keep in the forefront of my mind that a person could be in the audience who was on the verge of giving up on life and just needed one word of encouragement to keep them from falling off the edge. After you hit that "target" in preaching several times over the years, you get used to hearing "good job" or "you are powerful" or "God used you to bless my life." After years and years of preaching, you get to a place of being honored and respected in ministry. People will pay you "love offerings" to come and speak at their conferences.

There was a time I lived in Lafayette, LA, and a Catholic Church in Oakland, CA, wanted me to speak for their event. I told them I had relocated, and they said they still wanted me to

MISERY IN MINISTRY

come. They paid for my airfare, hotel, and gave me an honorarium. I was literally paid to come back to my hometown to preach the gospel in a church that I'd never set foot in. It was also a denomination I didn't know much about. My name had made it to the ear of someone who knew someone who thought I was valuable enough to pay to come back to the Bay Area to speak for them.

I've been invited to retreats that were held at beautiful resorts. I was able to bring a couple of people with me to assist me and to enjoy the vacation house they put us in for the night. At that same retreat, my honorarium was doubled at the last minute to stay an extra day to speak again with all expenses paid. I have spoken at conferences where there were hundreds of people crying at the words I was speaking because it confirmed some things in their lives or things they have experienced, and the words gave them hope. I have been preaching, and people have run to the platform or altar and put hundreds of dollars at my feet as I spoke because they felt like they were "sowing a seed" because the word I was giving them was that valuable to them.

I went to minister at one church, and there was a waiting area downstairs from the main sanctuary. During that time, I was mentally preparing to go speak before a crowd of people who were there to hear me as the special guest for the day. Usually, during that time, that's when the "business" of ministry is taken care of. I was given a 1099 to fill out because the offering was going to be over a certain amount that required the ministry to notify the IRS. I was to stay there until it was close to the time for me to be escorted to the platform/pulpit. When that time came, I was walked to an elevator by one of the church staff members along with my adjutant. It was surreal. I've preached at many places over the years but never at a place that had an elevator.

I felt like a rock star that was about to perform before an arena of people who paid good money to come to see me. It was far from rock star status, but having experiences like that can put you in a different headspace. It can have you thinking more highly of yourself than you are if you don't stay grounded. I preached and completed my assignment and was received well by the congregation. I was compensated well and was told that I could come back and speak for that church at any time, but I never did.

Experiences like that over time can make you feel entitled. You start to have what they call a "standard" when it comes to your ministry, and you should start expecting to be treated a certain way. Celebrities have riders. A rider is their list of demands they expect to have at a venue that they are coming to perform. Well, those same things happen in ministry. The venue representative will ask if there is anything you need to make you comfortable before or after you speak. They will ask if you have a preference for food or snacks in the room assigned to you as your personal space to prepare to speak before you come out to the pulpit.

Over time, I realized that I was very sensitive spiritually

when I had to preach. I didn't like a lot of conversation or commotion around me before I had to preach. As a lady, I didn't like to drink out of a bottle of water in the pulpit. I don't know why, but it just made me uncomfortable. But instead of demanding the venue provide me with a glass, I always had my own. Well, I didn't have it, but rather my adjutant or assistant would always have it for me.

That was another perk of ministry. Once you preached and traveled enough in ministry, you start to develop a team of people who will travel with your events. I never requested my assistant do these things. At some point in ministry, she realized I needed to have my own glass because she felt that not everyone cleans their glasses properly. And to be honest, she was right. The last place I preached for — prior to her bringing my own water, glass, and tea kit — I was given a dirty glass. I could see that the glass was dirty, so I didn't drink from it. From that point on, whenever I was asked if I needed anything or if I required any specific tea or beverage for preaching, I would gracefully decline and let them know that we would be bringing our own supplies. My assistant, Tiffany, coined the phrase that we were a "self-sufficient ministry."

One of the other perks I experienced was having a deacon from my church who would go to the venue before me to check things out. He would find out where my changing room was and where I was supposed to park. He would call me after he confirmed everything and ask me how far away I was from the venue and to inform me that he would be outside waiting for me when I pulled up. When I pulled up, he would direct me to my designated parking spot and take my bags and escort me to my changing area. If there wasn't a designated parking spot, I was to leave my car double-parked, he would take my bags to my changing room and go back and park my car.

Being a female in ministry, I always allowed the men to treat me like a lady. I always taught the women in the ministry that we were diamonds, so I made sure I was a lady and allowed the men to be gentlemen in ministry. I knew that once I was in preaching mode, I was very strong and bold in my delivery, but I always intentionally remained gentle and soft while the brothers in the ministry served me. Never did anyone cross any lines. There was never anything funny about them serving me. I always kept in the back of mind what Dr. Lela Edwards told me, "Step to the mic like a lady and then preach like you are crazy!" I reserved all of the boldness to stand before all of the different spirits I would face as a female preacher.

It was very humbling to be served in that manner. I never took people for granted and the things they did for me. I was the recipient and was being served. I saw what they were doing as a ministry and their service to God by serving His servant. I respected their ministry. People cooked for me. They made sure I was comfortable. They changed my shoes from heels to flats. They made my tea. They helped me change from sweaty clothes after I preached into dry clothes. They made sure I was safe getting home. They genuinely cared for me. I could never take them for granted. I could never feel like they were "supposed" to serve me. I valued and appreciated everything that was done for me. If you aren't careful, you can get caught up in the accolades and the praises of people.

I was "advancing" and "climbing" up the ministry scale, but I had to make a decision to live or to continue to be the "powerful anointed preacher" that the people loved. I was hurting so badly in my personal life that I literally wanted to die. I contemplated suicide. I tried to commit suicide, but it didn't work. After the original wedding date for Roy and I didn't happen, I was ready to check out. I thought I didn't want to live. I didn't know how to keep preaching and keep fighting for my life.

I was still serving as the pastor of Prophetic Worship Center and District Elder of the AAF Western District while married to but separated from Roy. After the formal wedding was canceled, I tried to keep pastoring. I tried to keep preaching. I started seeing a therapist. I was put on Zoloft to help me with my depression and thoughts of suicide. The best way I could describe Zoloft is the Botox of emotions.

The therapist wanted me to take off of work for a few weeks. I told her that work wasn't the problem and that I wanted to continue to work. I would take Zoloft, go to work and feel numb, and come home and sleep on my couch. I was emotionless. I could do my job, but I would have no feelings or emotions when I came home. I stopped sleeping in my bed for a while because it was hard for me to sleep in the bed, and he was no longer there. I was numb. My days ran into each other. I would go to work, come home and sleep on the couch. My life was on a slow repeat.

Even though I was taking Zoloft for depression, I still had to preach. I would go to church and preach, and surprisingly, that's when I felt most alive. I felt like I was preaching to save my life. After I preached, I would go back to feeling numb again. I knew that feeling was off. Even though I felt somewhat normal while preaching, I could tell I was trying to rescue myself. After I preached, I literally had no feeling. I knew this wasn't normal. I knew I couldn't go on too much longer like this.

Friends and family come to my house to pray for me. One night, my mother, my sister, Claudette, and ministry friend, Pastor Renee Winston, came and sat on my living room floor while I laid on my couch. They talked to me, encouraged me, and prayed for me. I wanted to feel better. I wanted my life to be different. I wanted to snap out of this fog. But I was damaged. I was hurting, and although prayers were going forth on my behalf, I just couldn't seem to shake the fog. I no longer wanted to die, but I wasn't sure how to live.

Nothing in ministry had prepared me for this fog I was in. I was stuck in a place of time. I was stuck between death and survival. The only way I knew how to fight was to let go of something — I had to let go of the church. I didn't want to. I loved preaching. I loved ministry. I served faithfully with my gifts and talents and money, so I reached out to my bishop.

I had served my bishop as the District Elder, traveling in and out of state to support his vision, and our church made sacrifices to attend multiple events at his church. He was supposed to be the pastor's pastor. Yet, when I needed him, he wouldn't return my calls.

He abandoned me in my time of need. I didn't know what else to do. I wanted to live. I had a son who loved me. I had a family who loved me. Although I felt death breathing down my neck, I knew there was more life in me to live. I had to make a decision. I had to do it quickly. Nobody would come to my aid. Nobody would listen. Peers in ministry thought it was something I could just preach my way through. I was drowning in despair. I didn't want to throw in the towel, but in order to live, I had to. I had to close the doors of Prophetic Worship Center so that I could live. I chose to live. I chose to step away from the pulpit, running revivals, and going to conventions and conferences to fix my life.

BROKEN PROMISES

As much as I tried to hold on to my second marriage, I just couldn't. It wasn't because I didn't want to. It was because he admittedly wasn't strong enough to stay focused on being a better person. Even after the separation, we reconciled. Once we reconciled, we were able to pull off the beautiful big wedding we initially planned. I probably should say that I was able to pull it off. It was a lot of planning, preparation, finances, and support from my family and friends that made sure the day was beautiful.

My vision was to make the day as special as possible for him. At the time, I had a "savior" complex, so I wanted everyone else to be happy. I wanted him to have a special day. I wanted him to be honored. I wanted him to look good in the eyes of others. I know people attended in full support of me who didn't believe he deserved it, but in my heart, I felt like he did because

I loved him so much. Literally, every aspect of the wedding was supported by my family, my friends, and my ministry connections.

His siblings decided they weren't going to attend the wedding because I didn't have his sisters as bridesmaids. Due to our "off and on" situation, I'd already had my bridesmaids established from the first wedding that was called off. Dresses, flowers, and plans had already been put in motion, and I didn't want to start all over. My other reason for not having them in the wedding was because I had specifically chosen each lady to be by my side for a reason. It wasn't just to have a "wedding party." These ladies stood by me during the trenches of my life, and I wanted them standing with me on that day. Their threats of not attending the wedding for that reason was ridiculous to me. Here we are in our forties, and I just refused to entertain that type of behavior.

One day, he drove me to the park down the street from our house, and we had a serious talk. He told me if his sisters couldn't be in the wedding that there would be no wedding. I was like, really? After everything I've done for you when nobody else was there for you, including your sisters and the rest of your family, you think you are going to threaten me with not having a wedding? I let Mr. Willis know there will be a party even if there is no wedding!

We were already married. The wedding was a celebration of our first anniversary. I deserved a party after being a prison wife, standing in lines to visit him, taking long drives before the sun came up, eating vending machine food, dealing with my personal belongings being searched, and being on lockdown with him for family visits. If he didn't want to show up as a protest to stand with his siblings in solidarity, then he didn't have to show up, but my family and friends and I were going to have an amazing party!

Needless to say, we had a beautiful wedding and a beautiful party. At the last minute, his siblings decided to attend. His brother refused to be his best man and had his "godbrother" stand in his stead. I had to shuffle the seating chart at the last minute to accommodate them, but I made it happen. I also listed all of the groomsmen as best men on the program instead of just the replacement best man. It was a hassle to get to that day, but we did it. I have no regrets. That was the day I gave him. Among so many other things I gave him, I gave him a day where he could shine and be celebrated. It was something he never experienced. He was also able to have a beautiful mother and son dance. I know that day meant the world to him. Sadly, his mother passed, but I'm so thankful for all of the blood, sweat, and tears that were shed to get to that day. Even if, in the end, it was only to give him that memory with his mother, it was worth it.

The wedding celebration was on December 21, 2014, and on April 8, 2015, he was arrested and went back to prison. I was devastated and felt betrayed. He was committing crimes while I was working hard to provide for our family. I had already closed the doors of the church, so this was time I was taking to focus on our marriage. We were supposed to be a family and working on goals together. However, the distractions of the streets and old running buddies got the best of him and led him back to illegal activity.

The night he was arrested, he had just left the house. He said he was going to see a friend and would be right back. Little did we know the sheriff's department was about to raid our house. We were being watched. He left and drove to the end of the block and was immediately surrounded by police cars and unmarked cars. My phone rang, and it was the deacon who used to go to my church. He and his wife just happened to be going to grab something to eat before they went to bible study at the church they started attending after our church closed. It was about two miles down the street from my house.

They drove up as the police were surrounding him. "Hey, Pastor! The police just pulled Roy over, they have him on the ground, and guns were drawn on him!" he said.

"Huh? He just left the house!" I said.

"We were at the light, and he made a U-turn, and they pulled him over. We're right here at the corner!" he said.

I was frantic and confused. Still, on the phone with the deacon, I ran down the stairs and started walking towards the end of the block. I saw several police cars and a black SUV. The SUV pulled off, and an officer got in my car that Roy was driving and drove off. I was screaming on the corner, "That's my car! Where are you going?" I started walking back towards our apartment complex and noticed the police cars making a U-turn.

They were coming to the house. The officer driving my car and another police car drove to the back of the dentist's office that was next door. An officer walked up to me and asked me if I was Kecia Willis. I said, "Yes." He said, "Your husband is being detained, and so are you!" I had no idea what was going on, and he could tell that I was visibly confused and scared.

"What? Why am I being detained? For what?" I asked. It felt like I was having an out of body experience. Nothing was making sense to me.

The officer started questioning me and asking me how long I had known "this guy." He asked what I really knew about him and if I'd known about his past. I told him that I'd known him for almost five years, we met at church, I'd known his family for many years and that he went to prison, that we had gotten married, and he's been out and completed his parole. The more the officer questioned me, the more he saw that I had no idea what was going on or knowledge of the crimes my husband was accused of committing.

He told me that they were waiting on a judge to sign a search warrant for my car and apartment, and as soon as they got word, they would be searching both. He asked if I had any concerns about it, and I told him no. I didn't know what they were looking for and why they were there, so I had nothing to hide. If they were looking for something dangerous, I wanted them to find it!

The search warrant was granted, and they went in to search the apartment. My mother lived in the same complex, so I went to her apartment while we waited for them to search. To this day, my mother still references that look on my face. She said it was a look on my face she had never seen in her life. She described it as blank. The only way I could describe it was that I was numb. I was so scared and confused that I went numb. There was no expression on my face or in my eyes. I didn't cry. I wasn't mad. I was just numb.

More officers stood around me as the other officer continued to ask me questions. Questions I didn't have answers to. I didn't know the name of his friend he was going to see. I didn't know the real name of one of his friends he always talked to on the phone. They always used street names. Not only did I not know their names, but I also couldn't identify them if they were to walk up on me today. He didn't take me around his friends, and he didn't bring them to the house. You could see the other officers were watching me closely to see if I were lying. I cooperated with the officer and told him everything I knew, which was very little.

After about an hour or so, they finished searching the apartment and the car. They let me go back in. Sure enough, just like the movies, everything was flipped up, over, and upside down. They were looking for a gun and a specific knife. They took one of my kitchen butcher knives but didn't find a gun. They stepped on picture frames and pulled clothes out of the closet. They unzipped the garment bag that my wedding dress was kept in and pulled the dress out of it. I guess they thought that was a good place to hide a gun. They gave me a document that was a list of items they had taken from the house and car. They took the knife, some clothes, a hat, and a pair of shoes.

My mother came back to my apartment to help me clean it up. I stood in a place that was once our home that was now in shambles. It was representative of our relationship and our marriage. As much as I tried to keep it clean and keep it together, it was ruined. It was trashed and destroyed. At that point, I knew I was done. I couldn't do it anymore.

When he was released from San Quentin in 2013, I told him I would never go back to prison with him. As much as I loved him, I couldn't stand to see him in prison again. He promised he wouldn't do that to me. He promised me he would never go back. He broke his promise, and he left me to clean up the mess in the apartment and clean up the mess he had made in my life. That day he slapped me on my butt, kissed me goodbye, and walked out of the house. That was the last time he walked out of my life. And that was the last time I saw him.

My family was very concerned about me. They knew how hard I took the last break up and they didn't know how I would handle this situation. Although I was hurt and devastated, I told God, "This time I want to live." I asked God for strength and courage to pick up the pieces of my life and move forward. It wasn't easy, but I have to give God all of the credit for getting me through it. I didn't know what my future was going to look like, but I knew I had one. I knew there was more life to live, and I just had to take it day by day.

I moved out of the apartment and moved in with my brother and his family. Oddly, I moved to the city he had moved to when he left me to stay with his children. As I drove around the city, I would often wonder if he had been to this store or had he gone to this gas station. I would recall different conversations we had when he would tell me a gym he was at with friends or a restaurant he was on his way to. There were many times I felt like I was retracing his steps. Even though it was weird for me to be in the city he lived in without me, I was determined to rebuild my life.

During that time, my brother allowed me to live with him and his family. I still had my job so I could contribute to their household financially and help as much as I could; I paid the rent on time, I paid extra bills, I bought food for their family, and I cooked and cleaned for a family of seven to show my gratitude to them for allowing me to stay there while I regrouped. I came to learn that my brother's (now ex) wife, the very person who I supported, pastored, and cared for at crucial times in her life, was very jealous of me. I was down at my lowest point and just trying to figure out my next steps in life, but she was jealous.

I had to file bankruptcy. During the process, I had to give up a car and get a new one. She didn't understand how business works and to use bankruptcy to reorganize finances, so she was angry at me for getting a new car. She said to me, "How can you get a f*&^%$# new car and you are living with someone?" They didn't have a new car. She wasn't working and had no life outside of having children, so I guess she hated me for being a working woman. That argument turned into her physically attacking me. That night she put me out of "her" government-assisted house where I was paying rent.

I drove down the highway at midnight with my car packed with boxes and clothes and cried. Once again, I was hurt, but I told God that I trusted Him. I told God that I had no idea what He was going to do in this situation, but I believed Him. I told Him I wanted to live. Things were looking grim again, but I wanted to live. On that dark highway on that dreary drive to my mother's one-bedroom apartment as my refuge, I was making a declaration that I wanted to live!

I lived in my mother's living room for a couple of months until a cousin let me rent a room from her back in the same city I was living in with my brother. My life was really like a ping pong game for several months. I left San Lorenzo, where I lived with Roy, moved to Antioch with my brother, went back to San Lorenzo to live with my mother, and moved back to Antioch to rent a room from my cousin. Thankfully, I had let go of everything except clothes and books, so I didn't have any furniture to store or move back and forth. I didn't even have a bed. Life became very simplistic for me. I would visit different churches in search of healing, but I didn't want to preach or be in ministry. I needed to be fed. I needed to sit and be replenished.

I found a church in the city. The Fellowship Church. It was a large enough ministry that I could sit in the pews and blend in the crowd. I wasn't known there, and they didn't want anything from me. I could go and worship and cry out to God and leave. Their motto was "Hope and Healing," and that was exactly what I needed. They offered small groups and invitations to serve in the ministry, but I didn't need that. I just needed to be restored. I was so broken, and I knew it. If I wanted to preach at any time, I could have called up a friend in ministry to arrange that. When you have a rapport in ministry, that's easy to do. But I didn't want to preach. I didn't need that type of attention or accolades. My heart was broken, my spirit was heavy, and my soul needed healing.

My son lived in Maine at the time, so I didn't have anyone to take care of. I believe God allowed me this time to focus on myself. I started working out and meal prepping. Taking time to care for my mind, body, and soul was the self-care I needed. It was an intentional effort. I never realized that self-care shouldn't be an afterthought. During this time, I began to heal from the inside out. I began to develop a glow. That glow became attractive.

After filing for divorce, I did the sneaky Facebook move of slowly removing pictures of us from my page. I didn't announce what happened. I didn't talk about his arrest or put all of our issues on social media. I just stopped talking about him and posted pictures of my current life and positive quotes. Of course, my family and close friends knew the situation. Others

MISERY IN MINISTRY

only knew that we were no longer married. And still, others were trying to figure things out. The glow started attracting the men. I started getting inbox messages. Some were legit and nice words of encouragement. Others were initial inquiries to hook up.

I never dated men in ministry, so I didn't know the game. I soon learned. Apparently, after the initial show of interest, the way the brethren try to get you on the "hook" is to talk about how it's time for them to settle down and find a wife. They will tell you how beautiful you are and how they could see you being an asset to their ministry. They talk about how smart and sexy you are and how you could offer them so much both naturally and spiritually. It's a game and a ploy! Being naïve to the church game, I didn't realize they were saying how much I could benefit them and how little they had to offer me.

There were two bishops I encountered during this time. They both played the same game. They both told me how they could see me as their wife. They both told me how they could see me being an asset to their ministry. They both wanted to be discrete about the potential of what was supposed to be a relationship. And as you can probably guess, they both had other women they were telling the same thing.

I wasn't dating both at the same time. But my experience with both of them was very similar. One of them invited me to his beautiful home and had me walk all through it and told me this could be mine. He literally had me walk through every room of the house and the backyard and said, "Every place the soles of your feet touch could be all yours!" He was corny and a bit controlling. I think he thought his wealth was so impressive that a woman would take whatever he dished. I wasn't even that attracted to him, but I was honestly contemplating going for it just because I was renting a room from my cousins at the time.

I even had a conversation with a friend at work and told him I might just go for it, settle for being with him for stability, and forget about love. He said, "You wouldn't do that, Kecia. You're not that type of person." He was right. But I figured, if ole bishop wanted to play games, I would too. Thankfully, I wasn't that desperate, and I didn't settle for waiting on men to decide to choose me or not. I had some vulnerable moments, but I pulled myself together and continued to glow.

FAVOR

Determined not to sit around and wait for a man to "pick me," I continued to focus on my glow up. I traveled, took myself out to dinner, and enjoyed my own company. Being a regular on social media, I would post selfies when I felt pretty and especially when I was all dolled up to go hang out. Positive quotes and words of affirmations became my choice to post when I was feeling down. It was my reminder that my current situation wouldn't always be this way and to have faith for brighter days to come.

One day while at work, I had to do a bank run. I exited the elevator while scrolling through my phone as I walked through the lobby. Suddenly, I yelled out, "no!" I leaned on the wall gasping for breath. The security guard asked if I was okay, and I responded no. I just read on Facebook that a friend of our family had passed. I was in disbelief! Not Kellye! No, no, no.

This just didn't make any sense. I messaged her nephew to confirm what I read in my timeline. I simply typed, "Nooo," and he responded, "Yes." Her untimely death was a shock to so many people. Not only was it a shock, but it was painful. It made no sense. She had been experiencing some migraines, but nobody imagined she would go to bed and not wake up.

A few days later, I received a call from Kellye's sister Lanetta. We all used to attend Covenant Worship Center, and our families developed a bond through prayer and fellowship. We all served in ministry together at one point at Covenant. Lanetta traveled with me and assisted me in my early days of ministry. It didn't matter that we didn't see each other all the time or no longer attended the same church, our bond was such that if we ever called on each other, we would be there. Lanetta asked if I would be the expeditor at Kellye's Home Going service. She said the family really wanted me to do it. She knew that I was no longer pastoring my church, but she also knew my heart for ministry and the people I love. I told her that it's not something that I wanted to do. It wasn't that I didn't want to serve the family, but rather I didn't want to have to serve in this capacity because it was Kellye's funeral. I didn't want Kellye to be gone. However, because my sister asked me to serve, I told her that I would.

Kellye's funeral was one of the largest funerals I had attended in a long time. Hundreds of people came to celebrate her life and to say their final goodbyes. I didn't know her pastor who was the officiator for the service, so I made sure to arrive early to spend time with him and some of the other elders in the office before the service to make sure we followed his instructions to ensure her celebration of life was carried out as the family wished.

Although I wasn't actively pastoring a church or preaching in a pulpit, I never dismissed the call on my life. I know who I am, and despite how people saw me, I understood my relationship with God. I knew when He assigned me to a task that it had to be done. Kellye's Home Going celebration was definitely one of them. I didn't take it lightly. My heart was hurting because I lost a friend and sister in Christ. However, I had to focus because I had a job to do that day.

As the ministers gathered before the service, we discussed the order of the processional, the scriptures that would be read, and where we would meet in the back of the sanctuary before we entered. People were gathering as we were meeting. The door was opened to the office we were meeting in, and you could see people walking by. I can't remember if I had to leave the room for something, but on my way back to the office, an elder was walking towards me. He looked familiar, but I didn't recall his name. He said, "Hi, sis. Kecia! How are you?" I was trying to focus on getting back to the office to make sure I heard everything the officiating pastor had to say. "Hello, God bless you," I responded. He said, "You don't remember me. I'm Milton. From Covenant Worship Center. Your brother Jonathan baptized me." I had no idea who he was.

He looked vaguely familiar, but I really didn't remember

attending church with him. Covenant Worship Center had a nice size membership with multiple services, so that could be the reason I didn't remember seeing him around very much. It could be that we attended different services. I didn't want to be rude, but I was trying to stay focused, so I said, "Oh, okay! It's good to see you." And then, once again, I said, "God bless you" and rushed into the office.

The service was beautiful. It was hard to say goodbye to Kellye, but her family and friends gave her an awesome and memorable send-off. There were a lot of people there I hadn't seen in years, and it was so nice to see them. It was like a reunion of the church family who had branched off and went in different directions but came back for one common goal, to celebrate Kellye. This was so indicative of her life. Kellye had such a big personality and bright smile. She loved outreach, and she had a way of bringing people together.

After the service, people were fellowshipping and greeting one another while trying to make their way to their cars to get to the gravesite. On my way out, here comes the elder again, "Hey, Sister Kecia. It was really good to see you." He had on his black suit and clergy collar. I was not impressed, and neither was I interested in any conversation. I had on my clergy robe, but I had on a cute dress underneath it, and I was ready to take it off, toss it in the back seat of my car and head out.

Trying to remain in clergy mode, I smiled and once again said, "God bless you" and told Milton that it was good to see him too and to take care. I made my way through the crowd, headed to the parking lot, said a few more hellos and goodbyes, tossed my robe in the back seat, and drove off. I didn't go to the gravesite or the repast. I knew my emotional limits. I served as asked and went home.

It's not uncommon to get new friend requests on Facebook when you reconnect with people you haven't seen in a while. And of course, the elder requested to be my friend. I accepted his request. Not long after, he messaged me and said it was good to see me at Kellye's celebration and that I did a good job as the expeditor of the service. I told him it was good to see him as well. I thanked him for the compliment and told him that it wasn't something I really wanted to do, but I had to be there to serve our sister. That was the extent of the dialogue. At least it was for the time being.

As life went on, I continued to post my selfies and positive quotes. One day I saw a picture of Facebook that simply read FAVOR. It was in bold letters with a bronze and gold background. I needed favor. I wanted favor. So, I made it my cover photo. I was no longer in a relationship with the bishop or the other bishop. In keeping up with my glow up, I continued to go to dinner and enjoy events solo.

The Golden State Warriors were doing well that year, and they were in the playoffs. After work, I would go "home" (to the house where I was renting a room from my cousin), change my clothes into my Warriors gear, and go to the local sports bar to have dinner and watch the game. It was always packed with Warriors fans, and it felt like hanging out with friends. I never knew anyone when I got there, but I would always meet people and have a lot of fun and then leave alone. I never went to try to hook up and never accepted a ride home with anyone. Occasionally, my brother or my cousin would come to hang out with me, but most times, I went alone.

I always checked in on Facebook whenever I would go somewhere alone. That was my way of letting my family know where I was and that I was safe. Just in case anything crazy happened, they would at least be able to track my location. I checked in that night I arrived at Tailgaters. People were commenting and telling me to enjoy the game, and fellow Warrior fans were chiming in on my post.

After a few minutes, I got a notification of a new comment. It was the elder. His comment said, "if I didn't have bible study tonight, I would join you." I read it and rolled my eyes. I thought to myself, *why?* but my nice and nasty, sarcastic response was, "Pray for me!" I had no idea why this man would invite himself to hang out with me. Clearly, I am not his type. His profile picture at the time was of him and his bishop. He had a Bible in his hand and was wearing a bow tie. Yeah... no, thank you, Sir! I don't think you would enjoy my company. I'm not that deep. I guess he went to his bible study, and I enjoyed my evening watching the Warriors.

A couple of weeks went by, and people were doing that Couples Challenge on Facebook. That's when they post pictures of themselves and tag other couples to do the same. I watched my married friends post over and over. I watched them post various pictures, and some of them were pictures they had taken at my last wedding! I had bridesmaids from the wedding tagging each other and other married friends. They all knew I was divorced, so they respectfully didn't tag me. I was feeling left out. My feelings were a little hurt.

Since all these couples were posting things, I shared a picture that was circulating of a really handsome man and said it was is for my single friends since all these married couples posting all of their lovey-dovey pictures and we didn't have to be left out. It was funny, and a lot of my single friends seemed to get a kick out of it. They enjoyed the photo of the handsome man and my sarcasm. We went back and forth, commenting and having a good time. It was all ladies, laughing and making jokes.

Then all of a sudden, there was a notification. The elder chimed in. He said he felt some kind of way as well about the couples' challenge, but he knew the Lord was going to bless him soon. "Ummm, ok sure," was my sarcastic thought. I was wondering why he was the only man on this post commenting. But once again to be nice, I simply "liked" his comment.

Once I shared that photo, I decided to change my status to "divorced" so that people wouldn't think I was still married posting something like this. I was never concerned about updating my status on Facebook before that. I guess I just felt like those who know already know, and those who need to know will know when I tell them. However, at that moment, I was concerned about the image, so I updated my status.

PING! Almost as soon as I changed my status to divorce,

the elder was in my inbox! He said, "I didn't know you were divorced." I told him, "Yes, I was... I just hadn't updated my status." He told me that he was divorced as well. We were chatting and having a basic conversation about being divorced.

Although my previous marriage didn't work, anybody who knew about our marriage, knew that I loved him and tried to make it work, but he just didn't value the woman I was.

I was rambling at that point and just being matter of fact. At that point, I was basically tooting my own horn, but I wasn't doing it to impress him. I started thinking about the good woman I know I am and how my ex didn't value me, so it was more like I was venting to him. After some back and forth conversation, he asked if he could take me out to dinner "from time to time" to get to know me. Whoa! Wait... what? Thankfully, this conversation was through messenger, so he couldn't see my facial expression. I had to go to his page to look through his pictures and check him out. I did a quick scroll through trying to see who he really was and what he was really about.

I know the elder is NOT trying to push up! I just know the elder is NOT trying to get at me! Ah naw... nope, nope, nope! Not another lying church dude. All this was running through my head. I guess I took too long to respond, so he wrote back, "I know you are a praying woman, so pray about my last question and let me know." I literally laughed out loud. I wrote him back and said that I didn't need to pray about going out to dinner and that it would be fine. However, I was thinking that he didn't ask me out for a date, he asked me on several dates at one time. He asked to take me to dinner "from time to time." He gave me his phone number and told me that he would like to have a phone conversation with me. I told him that would be fine. He then asked for my number and said he would prefer to call me first because that was just the man in him. HEY ELDER! Now I'm intrigued...

The next day he texts me and politely asked what time would be a good time to talk. I told him to call me during my lunch. That way, if I didn't like the conversation, it would be easy for me to get him off the phone, and I could use going back to work as an excuse. He called me, and surprisingly we had a wonderful conversation. I was shocked at how much we actually had in common. I would have never known the elder, and I had so much in common.

Both of our fathers were deceased. We were both frustrated about things we saw taking place in ministry. We had both been married more than once. We were both in the rebuilding stage of our lives. We were both at work at the time, so we couldn't talk too long. However, the conversation was definitely worth continuing, so we decided to hang up and talk more later that evening. That was July 20. I needed a friend that day. It was the anniversary of my father's death, but after talking to Milton, my day was brighter.

We talked every day throughout that week. He shared some goals and plans he was looking to accomplish. We talked about past relationships and marriages. I really enjoyed talking to him.

He was a lot more laid back than I perceived from the bow tie, bishop, and bible profile picture. Towards the end of the week, in one conversation, we started talking about dating and the games people play.

I told him about my past experiences with the bishops and how I had no interest in anyone who wanted to play games. I explained to him that I would rather a man tell me that he wanted to be a ministry associate or a prayer partner instead of acting like he wanted to be married just to get close to me.

I didn't know it at the time, but this man had things on his mind very early on after he saw me at the funeral. He had been watching my page. He had been looking at my pictures — all of them. He saw how I treated myself. He saw my positive vibes. He saw that I did not once berate my ex on my page. He saw me as his "pretty girl."

Milton was different from anyone I'd met. He was very direct and upfront about what he wanted. He told me over the phone that he wasn't trying to be a prayer partner or a ministry associate. He said, "I'm trying to holla!" I was shocked! He went from being "the elder" to Milton! Milton did not come to play any games. He told me that he was trying to holla!

Since that was established, I knew how to have a conversation with him, knowing that he was, in fact, interested. That Friday evening, I had plans to have dinner with my mother. We were celebrating my promotion at work. Milton was telling me about some great things that were happening in his job, and I was happy for him. I didn't know if I was supposed to be impressed or not. I was happy for him, but I was really focused on my own promotion. Later, I realized he was trying to impress me, or at least show me how he could provide for me.

I had dinner with my mother in San Lorenzo and made my way back to Antioch. It was after 9 p.m., and I was on BART since I had left San Francisco to meet my mother for dinner. He was kind enough to talk to me on the phone while I was heading home. I figured it was the end of the week, and it would be nice to see him in person sometime that weekend.

When I asked him if he had plans, he told me that his friends were talking about going fishing. I was somewhat taken aback. I thought he would have made plans to see me the way he was talking. He was starting to seem like just another guy who pretended to be interested and then came up with excuses. "Oh, ok," I said to him. I tried not to let the disappointment come out in my tone. He made sure I made it home safely. We said goodnight.

Within moments we were back on the phone. He said, "Let me ask you a question. What would it take to be your man?" I was caught off guard by his question. I thought we were done with chatting for the night, especially since he told me he was considering going fishing with his friends. Trying to be coy and thinking that I could hold off on answering the question, I responded, "I think that's a conversation we should have in person." To my surprise, he asked, "Where are you right now?"

"Wait! Wait! I wasn't ready!"

"What do you mean?" he asked. "What's your address? I'll

come to you right now."

Oh, lawd! I started stuttering and scurrying around my little room. I told him you can't come over here now.

He wouldn't take no for an answer. I said, "Okay. If you come over, you can't come inside. I'll meet you outside." He said, "Text me the address, and I'll see you in a few minutes." Thinking I was in for the night, I had to jump up and put on something cute. He didn't know what I was really working with the last time he saw me. I had on that preaching robe that covered up all the goods. I grabbed some nice fitting jeans and a cute top, brushed my teeth, and sprayed a little perfume. This wasn't the elder coming over, this was Milton, and he wasn't coming to play. He had questions, and he wanted answers tonight!

He called me when he pulled up and told me he was outside. I had no idea what I was going to say to him, but I was happy to see him. Our conversations were so meaningful, and we connected so well over the phone, it felt like we had known each other for years. However, I was still a little nervous to see him so unexpectedly. When I went outside, he was standing at the end of the driveway. I walked up to him, and he held me. He didn't just hug me. He held me as if I belonged to him.

It felt like I melted in his arms. He asked me if he could kiss me, and I said, "Yes," and he did! After we kissed, I turned my back to him, and he pulled me back close to him. He wrapped his arms around my shoulders, and I wrapped my arms around his muscles. I laid my head back on his shoulders. We both looked up at the stars. We sat outside and held each other. It was a warm, starry night in July. At that moment, we just knew we belonged together.

Although I never did actually answer his question that night, it became clear that we were going to start dating. We talked about who we had been dating or casually talking to and making sure we were upfront with each other about not being in any other relationships in any way, shape, or form. Although neither of us were dating at the time, we felt like it was the right thing to do to inform those "potentials" that we had found someone who we were going to commit to. Some people deserved to be notified. For others, we agreed that the ones we only spoke with occasionally would be told whenever they reached out by phone, text, or otherwise.

I appreciated his honesty with me. He was serious about being with me and didn't want to play games. I hadn't met anyone like him in a long time. It was so refreshing to meet a man who pursued me, who was upfront about his intentions and honest enough to act upon them. We soon realized that at our age and based on our experiences, we didn't want to be without each other. He said my cover photo on Facebook caught his attention. He had been talking to God about favor. The type of favor that accompanies a wife.

> "The man who finds a wife finds a treasure,
> and he receives favor from the LORD."
> -Proverbs 18:22

I happen to post FAVOR, and he found me. When he found me, I didn't have to get myself together to be a wife. I was already a wife. My diamond was shining, and it wasn't hard for him to find his treasure in me.

He met my family. He met my grandmother, and she told me that he was the one! My grandmother doesn't play when it comes to her family, and she will tell you if she discerns something is wrong or off about a person. She gave her blessing. After she gave her blessing, we posted a picture of us together on Facebook and changed our statuses to "In a Relationship." That caught a lot of eyes and attention. Especially for those who didn't even know I was divorced.

We decided to be in a relationship in July, knowing we wanted to get married. We started playing with the thought of getting married in November. When I talked to my grandmother again, she said, "Whatever you are going to do, do it in a hurry." I knew what she meant. He knew what she meant. In other words, Granny was saying, November is too far away. So, we didn't play any games.

We had an intimate, relaxed backyard wedding with about 50 family members and friends. We comfortably got married in jeans and white shirts because that's what we wore when we went to church together for the first time. We asked our guests to be comfortable and wear the same thing. It was simple. It was special. We were married on August 27, 2016. Forty-four days after our first in-depth inbox conversation on Facebook.

DEMONS RESURFACED

In the early days of our marriage, Milton worked out of town a few days a week. He would be gone for two or three days and then home a couple of days and back on the road. I admired him for being a trucker. I think it's pretty cool to actually know someone and be married to a man who can handle those eighteen-wheelers. He would be away, but we would talk all the time. Having such a short courtship, we remained in the honeymoon phase for a while. He explained to me the conditions he had to deal with being on the road. At that time, he slept in his truck and showered at the rest stops. The bathroom accommodations weren't always the best.

I knew he was toughing it out on the road. When he came home, I wanted him to be able to relax and be comfortable. It was important to me to make sure he had a home-cooked meal when he came home. The house had to be cleaned, and it had to smell fresh. I wanted him to know that when he came home, he could leave the road on the road and just relax and enjoy a peaceful home and me, his treasure.

I worked a full-time job and had a long commute to work. My commute was about an hour and a half to two hours each way daily. At the time, there wasn't a BART extension, so I had to do a bus transfer to the closest BART station. I had a full day, but I never used that as an excuse to slack on doing what I felt were my responsibilities as a wife. Milton didn't require of me as much as I put on myself. However, I felt so grateful to have a husband who was on my same level financially and had the same work ethic. I never experienced that before, so I wanted to make sure I did everything I could to show my gratitude.

Early on in our marriage, family members needed help and needed a place to live. Milton said they could live with us because we had extra rooms. Since they were my family members, I felt especially responsible for making sure, no matter what, that he was still comfortable in his own home. I didn't mind being able to support family in their time of need, but I couldn't allow my new husband to sacrifice comfort when he worked such a strenuous job. I found myself cooking, cleaning, working, mediating, and making sure everyone was okay at all times. I got to the point of being burnt out, and I didn't even realize it. I was running on empty again.

We were newlyweds. Not only were we newlyweds but we didn't know each other very long at all before we got married. Forty-four days after a conversation through Facebook messenger and we were married. Our marriage became on the job training. We were teaching each other daily. The pressure of supporting family members began to weigh heavily on both of us. We wanted to help, but it was hard for us. We didn't even have a year married under our belt. Which meant we didn't even have a year of knowing each other under our belt before we took on supporting others. We hadn't experienced how to handle real pressure and stress together. We didn't have the full run of our house before we opened the doors for family to come live with us. As we began to experience life issues together, the pressure started building, and tension began to rise.

I felt like I owed him so much because he rescued me from a bad situation. Milton was my knight-in-shining-armor. It wasn't that I didn't have a good job or make good money, but when he came along, he showed me how to walk in faith again and to believe that God would open doors for us. I had been so devastated and broken in my previous marriage, then having to live with my brother and his family to living with my mother and then with my cousin, that I didn't think I could get a place of my own again — especially after filing bankruptcy. I thought it would take years to get back on track.

When he came into my life, he was a blessing and favor was upon us, and God opened door after door for us. I was afraid of losing again. I was afraid of loss. I didn't want to lose, so I held a lot of my feelings in. I kept my mouth shut and held a lot of things in that I should have been able to express to him. Once again, it wasn't that I couldn't talk to him. I just felt like it was easier to keep it to myself instead of speaking up to even have a conversation about our differences.

In our second year of marriage, I didn't know if we would make it. It became too exhausting. I was emotionally spent. I was trying to handle so much. I felt like I was trying to collect sand as it slipped through my fingers. We had constant disagreements. We had constant blow-ups. I convinced myself that we were living in the consequences of marrying too soon. There was a blessing in being found. However, the consequence of marrying so quickly was the lack of learning more about each other before committing to being married. We had a lot in common, but we also had a lot of differences that were starting to be revealed.

Milton is very headstrong about his beliefs and convictions, and I am as well. He had a perception of ministry that was different from mines. He helped pastor a church, and I had actually founded a church. The responsibilities and experience we had were very different. He constantly talked about launching Prophetic Worship Center again, and I told him I did not want to do that! I was adamant about not wanting to start a church again. I told him if he wanted to open a church, I would support him and be his first lady, but I didn't want to relaunch.

He kept pushing the issue of relaunching Prophetic Worship Center. He told me how he used to ask mutual friends about me when I was pastoring. I didn't even know he remembered me like that. The more I shared with him about the

MISERY IN MINISTRY

church when it was open, the more he wanted to relaunch. It became frustrating for me. I started resenting him.

One day, I was at the point of tears. I messaged him and told him that I was hurting because he wanted the church to reopen so badly, but I didn't want to. I explained how it hurt me because he should have found me sooner. It was like I blamed him for having to close the doors of the church. I told him, if you had found me sooner, you could have come to the church and helped me while I was going through a hard time, and we could be pastoring together now. I blamed him for waiting too long to find me, and now it's too late. I demanded that he stop pressuring me about the church. I was starting to unravel emotionally, and I didn't realize it.

Milton got us a dog, and that dog became my baby. Everyone who knows me knows that Ezra is my son. I cried when he was born, and I was the one who picked him up from the breeder when he was six weeks old. Ezra knows that I am his Mama! Ezra is a biblical name that means "help." He is my help and my protector. Milton trained him to protect me and not let anyone get too close to me.

Ezra understands that Milton is Daddy, but he watches him with a close eye when he's close to me. Milton trained him that way so that I would always feel safe, even with him. He knew that I had been in abusive relationships before and never wanted me to be afraid of him. So, he trained Ezra to protect Mommy even if Daddy gets out of line.

Ezra is my first dog. I never experienced the love and loyalty of a dog before. Although we have three sons as a blended family, we didn't have children together. Ezra became our child that we were raising together. We had differences about how to train him. I didn't know how to train him, but I knew that he was attached to me and that he would listen to me.

I was always the softy. I didn't want Milton to be too hard on him. We got him at six weeks; however, I did have the understanding that this dog was eventually going to get up to 150 pounds or more, so it was important to remain dominant over him at all times. It had to be established early who was the alpha dog (which was Milton) in the house. Milton played rough with him. I coddled him and trained him to be obedient about not going potty in the house, and not eating up shoes and furniture. The hard stuff was left up to Milton.

Milton is particular about certain things. Sometimes it's things that don't make sense to me. However, I realized when you marry someone in their forties, they are already set in their ways, and not too much was going to change about him. I understood that about him, but I didn't feel he held that same understanding about me.

Those extra steps I would have to take to do things his way would cause more work for me. Again, he didn't ask me to do things for him, but if I did, he liked it done a certain way. I tried to comply as much as I could to keep him happy. I just wanted him to be happy. Either I was going to do things for him or not. If I chose to do those things, I had to do them the way he liked it. It became frustrating. I knew how to multi-task and cut corners to get things done quickly, but again, he likes things the way he likes things.

We bumped heads in those areas. I wanted him to just shut up and see that I was getting things done even though they weren't his way. He felt like he didn't ask me to do it anyway. I felt that if it needs to be done, I'm the one that has to do it anyway, so just let me do it my way. It was never anything major. We just constantly bumped heads on processes and procedures of how to run the house and how to handle the dog.

Milton is loud. Lord have mercy. . . he is loud! He is loud when he's on the phone. He talks loudly when he's having a regular conversation. If he gets excited during that conversation, he gets even louder. It's almost impossible for us to be on our phones at the same time. I can never hear the person clearly on my phone because he talks so loudly on his phone. I didn't realize how his loud voice made me anxious. I would become irritated at times because he was so loud, but I didn't notice how it was making me jittery.

There were times I was enjoying a quiet evening at home watching a movie, and he would walk in the house yelling, "Kecia Taylor!" It would scare the hell out of me, and then I would be upset. He would look confused and say, "Did I scare you? Sorry." He meant no harm. His voice just carries so much, and it startles me if I'm not expecting him to walk in the room.

Milton spends time with Ezra doing drills. This is the time he takes with the dog to teach him how to be obedient or how to protect. He also teaches him commands. One day I was in the shower, and they were working on commands. Whatever Milton was trying to teach, Ezra was afraid, and he was running away. Just like a child, when Ezra runs from Daddy, he runs to Mommy. Ezra was running from Milton and ran to the bathroom where I was.

Milton was making a sound that he does with him that sounds like a scary monster sound. It was the commotion of Milton's loud voice, a 150-pound dog running, and Milton running behind him — I was trying to enjoy a relaxing shower, and all I heard was rumbling and chaos, and it was coming towards me. I screamed out, "STOP IT! STOP IT! LEAVE HIM ALONE! STOP IT!" I snapped. I couldn't take that sound any longer.

I got out of the shower, and Milton was upset because I yelled at him. He was trying to explain to me that he was working with the dog and that he needed to make sure Ezra understood he was in charge. I yelled at him, "IT'S NOT ABOUT THE DOG! IT'S NOT ABOUT THE DOG!" Milton had no idea what was wrong with me and couldn't understand what was going on. He stood his ground and said, "It is about the dog. I'm trying to train him and teach him that he has to obey me!" I screamed again, "SHUT UP! LISTEN TO ME! IT'S NOT ABOUT THE DOG! I CAN'T TAKE IT!"

I managed to gather myself for a moment and tried to explain to Milton that the sound of chaos, loud voices and commotion reminds me of when my father would come over to our house in the middle of the night, and we'd be awakened by my mother's screams because he was beating her. I don't like loud unexpected noises because it takes me back to that childhood memory. I was shaking, and I had to get away from Milton.

I got dressed and went to Lowe's. I just needed to get away from him so I could breathe. I was still in a fog. I hadn't felt that way in a long time. It was bad. I had slipped back into that dark place. He called me while I was walking the aisles of Lowe's. He had been doing some research online. He asked me if I thought I had PTSD (post-traumatic stress disorder). I had never heard of anyone who wasn't in the military who suffered from PTSD. I told him I didn't know about PTSD, but I knew something wasn't right. He suggested I call a therapist. I told him I would.

Milton and I are very different, although we have a lot of things in common. He addresses an issue, then it's over, and that's it to him. I need time to process it. Once, he called me and told me he thinks I need to see a therapist because he suspected I had PTSD. For him, problem identified, and problem solved. I, on the other hand, was still in a fog. I drove around town for a while, and all types of thoughts from my past and previous marriage started to surface. I don't even know why they came up. The thoughts I was having had nothing to do with the incident that had just occurred. But they were coming to the forefront of my mind.

When I got back home, Milton asked me if I was okay. I told him, "Yes," although I wasn't. He was leaving for work, and for some reason, he started asking me questions about his youngest son coming to live with us. I have no idea where this thought came from, but it was ironic because on my way home, I was thinking about how I had taken on the responsibility of taking in my previous husband's young sons on a whim without hesitation. I was thinking about how it would have been wiser to ask so many more questions before I allowed them to move into our home. It was weird that Milton would ask me that question. My response to him was, "I would have to ask a lot of questions and get clarity before that happened." I didn't say no. I was just saying I would ask questions and get an understanding. For some reason, he didn't like my response and felt like I was saying I didn't want him to move in. I'm still in a fog and struggling to process everything. I don't even understand where this question is coming from. His son's mother has made no indication that she would ever want him to come live with us, so I didn't understand where this hypothetical question came from and why my response was such a problem.

I was hurting, and I didn't have the emotional capacity to try to understand his perspective. He had just told me that he felt like I had PTSD. I didn't understand why he presented me with such a heavy hypothetical question when I came home. The fog got heavier. He left for work. Ezra and I were home alone. I slipped into that full-blown dark place. I started speaking out loud. No matter what I do, it will never be good enough. I can never do enough to make him happy. I can never do enough to make anyone happy. I'm tired. I've tried to be there for everyone, but nobody seems to care to be there for me. I'm done. I want out. Not just out of this marriage, I want out of this life.

I made a video telling my family goodbye. I talked to Ezra and told him that I love him so much and that he would always be my baby, but I had to leave him. I texted Milton and told him goodbye. He called me back and asked what I was talking about. I told him that I didn't want to live because I'm never good enough. He told me that he was going to call the police if I didn't call my family to come over. I kept stressing to him that I wanted to die. He said he would call the police, and if they came, they would have to shoot Ezra because Ezra wouldn't allow them to get close to me. I lost it even more.

Somehow the thought of the police killing Ezra stressed me out more than the pressure I felt about living. How could he say that? No! They can't kill my baby! I wanted to die, but I didn't want Ezra to die. My cry was more intense, and I was confused. How could I protect Ezra if the police came? How could I allow someone to come and rescue me? I needed help, but I didn't want my baby to get killed. The fog was so heavy.

He must have been texting my family at the same time because all of a sudden, they were at my door. My brothers Jonathan, Patrick, and my mother came in and rescued me. Ezra loves them, so it was no problem for them to come in and sit with me. I told them how I was feeling and that I was just overwhelmed. I felt like I was never good enough and was so tired. I explained my feeling of being in a fog, and I couldn't shake it. The longer they sat with me, the better I felt. They loved on me. They made me laugh. They prayed for me. They told me how much they loved me and needed me to live. My mother told me that I needed to call the doctor again. I agreed. She made me promise that I would. Before they left, I felt the fog lift. I felt like I would be fine; my mind was clear, and I no longer felt like I wanted to die... until I woke up the next morning.

THERAPY: A NEW BEGINNING

I AM A WORK IN PROGRESS. THE LAST TIME I EXPERIENCED being in a fog and wanting to commit suicide, I went to Kaiser, but I didn't follow through. I knew that I could get the help I needed if I committed to doing the work. I remembered the last time how devastated my son was when he knew I wanted to commit suicide. I didn't want to do that to him again. Although I needed to go get help for myself, I was still thinking about my family. I was thinking about how hurt they would be if I took my own life. I didn't want to cause them any pain. However, if I didn't get the help I needed, that's exactly what I would do.

I made an appointment and was quickly able to get in to see a crisis manager at the Kaiser Mental Health facility. I intentionally dressed casually and didn't get all dolled up. I had on a little makeup, but nothing fancy. I wanted to look presentable but not too fancy. I signed in and filled out the questionnaire. I checked the boxes to rate my feelings of depression, anxiety, and suicide. I checked the boxes to indicate that I didn't have any weapons and that I was not in an abusive relationship. I sat patiently and waited for my name to be called.

This gentle-looking African American man came out and called my name, "Kecia Willis." Man, I still hadn't updated my name with member services. This is already starting off weird. I wasn't expecting to hear that name. My name is now Taylor. Willis is my previous name and the name that reminds me of so much pain and disappointment. I walked into his office and sat down on the couch. I smiled and took a deep breath. As I started explaining to him the series of events that brought me in his office, he listened attentively. He was so kind.

I explained to him how I had only been married two years, and my husband just doesn't seem to understand how hard I work to make sure our home is clean and comfortable. I felt like he was nitpicking at everything and wasn't understanding me. I told him about the incident with Ezra and how I snapped. I just wanted my husband to understand how hard I'm trying and to be more sensitive to my needs, so I don't feel like I'm not good enough and want to check out.

The crisis manager sat back and began to talk to me. He was patient, and he allowed me to say everything I needed to say. Then he said something I will never forget. He said, "You are tricky. You are very well put together and articulate. You walked in like you had it all together, but you have a lot of demons to deal with." Huh? What? I was not trying to put on airs of any kind. I came to bear my soul and to get help. He continued, "I do believe your husband can be a little more understanding, but he doesn't sound like a bad guy. He researched information to try to understand what was going on with you. However, this isn't two years of issues; this is over forty years of unresolved issues that you need to address." Then he said, "Your husband was right; you do have PTSD." Well, stick a fork in me, I'm done!

My situation was so bad that he told me he could actually admit me into the hospital that day. But he felt like I had enough of a support system and wanted help that he wouldn't. It would be several weeks before he could get me scheduled with a permanent therapist, so he suggested I attend some PTSD group meetings. He also said that he wanted to see me for one more visit before he assigned me to a regular therapist.

I went to two group meetings before I saw him again. The meetings were helpful. Since my association with PTSD was only regarding military veterans, I was shocked to see people in the group who had never served in the military, but they had issues just like me. I heard stories of traumatic situations that had nothing to do with guns or explosions. These were people who had experienced bad or harmful things in their lives that caused them to seek help. These were people just like me.

In the group meetings, I learned PTSD causes anxiety when you have flashbacks about a traumatic situation. I also learned how to recognize "triggers." Triggers are events that remind you of a traumatic event of the past. Sometimes you don't even realize it, but your subconscious self does, and you react. I was taught tools on how to identify my triggers and to be aware of what I was thinking and feeling when it happened. I learned how to acknowledge my emotions of fear, anger, or sadness without allowing those same emotions to take me to a dark place.

When I saw the crisis manager again, he helped me to navigate through my thoughts and feelings. He helped me to understand how I am "present" when other people are around, but it's when I'm alone and left with my own thoughts that I have the biggest struggle. Those are the times I have to fight against the negative thoughts in my own head. I learned about cognitive distortion and my thinking errors.

Cognitive distortion is like thinking *I'm not good enough*. I learned how to have rational thoughts instead. A rational thought to counter "I'm not good enough" is "I am good enough even though I may have made a mistake this time." I taped examples to my refrigerator at home to remind me to exercise rational thoughts. I had to do the work and be intentional about healing my mind. I was determined to do what needed to be done to live.

I was eventually assigned to a regular therapist. I met with a psychiatrist who prescribed medication for anxiety. I needed medication to help me balance my jittery feelings and nervousness. He explained how the medicine would regulate my brain. The example was used that it's normal to be startled by a car that cuts you off in traffic, but then your nerves calm down once you realize you weren't in an accident. However, it's not normal to have that experience and be traumatized the rest of the day, continuing to worry about "what ifs" and going into thoughts of death and darkness as a result of what didn't even happen.

Those are the type of thoughts I often had. Along with PTSD, I had developed a phobia of driving long distances. I was nervous about driving on the freeway even thirty miles from home. I missed a lot of events because I didn't want to drive. I would always make up excuses, but my thoughts would tell me that I might get into a car accident. My father died in a car accident, so I was afraid it was going to happen to me. I was limited on where I would go. I would only drive locally and was nervous about riding in the car with anyone else. I had so much to work out and work through.

However, this time I committed to therapy. I committed to understanding my issues. I wanted to make sure I could manage my feelings and emotions regardless of what other people did. I didn't want to sink into that dark place based on anyone else's actions or behavior. I learned more about triggers and what that meant for me. I learned how to say, "No." I learned that I didn't have to be everything to everyone. I'm not always successful in this area, but it's something that I'm aware of that I have to continue to work towards.

I learned how to speak up for myself to Milton. It was an adjustment, but I learned how to speak my mind. In the beginning, to avoid conflict, I would hold back. But I had to learn how to have a difference of opinion or perspective without feeling guilty or feeling like our marriage couldn't survive because of our differences. This was a challenge. He would often say to me, "You've changed!" He was right. I *had* changed. I needed to express myself instead of keeping things bottled up so that I didn't internalize things and check out. I was changing, yet I was changing for the better.

I saw my therapist once a month for several months. Over time, she was able to see that I was utilizing the tools she was giving me, and my visits became more spaced out. I still have her as my therapist; however, I don't see her as much as I used to. I was given so many tools to fix my life that I still use to this day. I am an advocate for therapy.

If we are blessed to have medical benefits and insurance, then we should use the whole package. We shouldn't just go to the doctor for high blood pressure or diabetes and ignore our mental health. The treatment is available if we would use it. I'm not ashamed to go see a therapist or admit that I have one.

Therapy saved my life.

FINAL THOUGHTS

Accepting or acknowledging the call to ministry in your life is beautiful. It's a blessing to be chosen by God to make an impact in this world. However, if there are unresolved issues in your life, they could very well hinder your progress. And even if God allows you to progress in ministry with those unresolved issues, it doesn't mean that you don't need to get help to address them. It just means if you don't, you will eventually find yourself operating in ministry while being miserable or causing misery in the lives of those you are called to serve.

Do yourself a favor and get the help you need. Don't be ashamed. Get help and be made whole. You don't have to be in misery while in ministry.

www.ingramcontent.com/pod-product-compliance
Lightning Source LLC
Chambersburg PA
CBHW032126090426
42743CB00007B/485